TOWARDS A NEW ECONOMIC ORDER AND THE CONQUEST OF MASS POVERTY

LICHAUCO

Original Edition, 1986,
Alejandro Lichauco
Re-issue, 2017

"To the Memory of my father"

AUTHOR'S NOTE

This paper is the nucleus of a larger work which is in process of writing.

Incomplete as it is, this is being released for two reasons.

One is that, as is, the paper can stand on its own and contains enough materials to provide the basis for a working dialogue with, and among, groups and individuals, on a subject of primary importance.

The other is to influence the ongoing Constitutional Commission towards a new charter that would unleash three processes: the process of de-colonization; the process of industrialization; and the process of economic democratization.

I believe that only when these three processes are set in motion can Philippine society begin to wage serious war against mass poverty and reconstruct itself on a higher foundation.

The central purpose of this paper is to focus national attention to the problem of mass poverty and the need for a comprehensive approach to it through a new economic order that would confront and eliminate its roots and structural causes. Unless that problem is overcome, there can be no normalcy, and everything is peripheral.

I will appreciate receiving the critical comments and constructive suggestions of the reader, particularly concerning the proposals in Part Two, for possible incorporation in a final and larger version of this work.

Alejandro Lichauco
90-C 4th St, New Manila, Q.C.
Tel. Nos.: 70-19-86; 70-63-95
722-43-47

Part One

I. The Objective And Historical Setting Of The Poverty Problem

Introductory and Preliminary Remarks.

Framing a new constitution provides a people with the historic and momentous opportunity to reorganize their society on a new and higher basis for a better life.

The reorganization of Philippine society is now a compelling need. We have been a republic for the last forty years, and as a republic we have lived under two constitutions. But the condition of our people and the state of the nation, far from progressing, have progressively deteriorated, particularly over the last twenty years.

A decade ago, estimates were that 40% of our people lived below the poverty line. Today, estimates run as high as 85%.

Seven out of ten Filipinos are under-nourished.

Time was when undernourishment in Asia was synonymous with the impoverished and starving millions of China and India. Today, that term seems to have been reserved mainly for the Filipino. No one talks of the undernourished Chinese, the undernourished Indian or even the undernourished Indonesian.

In this "only Christian nation in Asia," mass poverty has forced children to prostitution in an alarming scale and the country is now a major world center for that particular perversion.

From published reports there are at least a

million Filipinas who, in a bid for survival, have submitted themselves for auction in today's white slave trade as mail order brides.

In the rural areas, home to 70% of Filipinos, our youths reach a maximum of only six years of schooling.

We have actually degenerated into a nation of undernourished bodies, enfeebled minds and impoverished sixth graders, living sub-human lives.

And what does sub-human living mean? It means, in the vivid description of Dom Helder Camara, the famed archbishop of Recife in Brazil, to live with no real home, on insufficient food, on indecent clothing, with neither health nor work, illiterate and without hope.

And as that good archbishop reminds us, "for anyone who lives in a state of under-nourishment, of chronic diseases, of ignorance and despair, everything atrophies, human dignity, intelligence, the sense of persona] freedom." (Camara, *Church and Colonialism,* 41, Sheed and Ward, 1969).

At least 40 million Filipinos are trapped in this sub-human living; which means that out of 55 million Filipinos only 15 million live in dignity and able to function as human beings should.

This is a society where the young have no hope for tomorrow; where parents must suffer the misery of their children, and agonize over the bleakness of their children's future; where the able-bodied must leave family and home in order to survive abroad; where the aged, the handicapped and the infirm must face life unaided; a society whose scientists, teachers, artists, civil servants, professionals and soldiers are either unemployed or underpaid, feel unneeded and unwanted; where one born poor, lives in ignorance and want, and dies poor.

One wonders where really lies its Christianity; or what is the meaning of Christianity in such a society, whose inhabitants are pathetic caricatures of a God in whose image they were supposed to have been born.

The human condition in the Philippines reflects the condition of its pre-industrial economy. It is backward, stagnant and dying; its science and technology primitive; its mines and waters fast being bled of their wealth; its forests denuded; its once fertile lands rendered barren by poisonous fertilizers.

Negros is the Philippines in microcosm.

The very terms under which the economy is to exist are dictated by a foreign government and the country's international creditors.

The nation is as enslaved by poverty as the individuals who comprise it.

This is a wretched land of wretched people.

We cannot endure indefinitely as a nation-state this way. We are destined to cease as a state, dismembered and devoured by more vigorous and stronger neighbors, unless the nation is reborn.

And it can be reborn only if the social scourge that has reduced 40 million Filipinos to modern-day servitude is eliminated, as it is being eliminated in the rest of Asia.

And it can be done.

The war against mass poverty can be won. It is being won all over Asia. Except in this country of 50 million Catholics consoled by a faith that human suffering purifies the soul.

But poverty has now assumed in this

country the dimensions of a social and spiritual disaster.

And not even the euphoria of February's events can conceal that.

Need to identify and focus on the real causes of mass poverty.

The war against mass poverty must begin by recognizing the true causes which, in the Philippine context, have bred and nurtured it

The reason is that unless we do, those causes will never be uprooted, and they will continue functioning undisturbed, as they have done so all these years. We shall be doing battle with factors that have no real connection with what we wish abolished, and moved to measures which do not really touch the problem.

Two examples suffice of prevailing theories which have misled and blunted the search for the correct remedies.

One is the theory that the mass poverty is due largely to overpopulation. No less than an internationally prominent Filipino, Mr. Rafael Salas of the United Nations, is identified with this thinking.

The silliness of this theory becomes evident simply by asking: if it were so, then why is the human condition in China, Japan, South Korea, Taiwan, not to mention the United States and the Soviet Union, and the rest of the developed countries, of a higher quality now than what it was fifty years ago when their respective populations were considerably smaller. The human condition in these countries should have deteriorated with the increase in their populations.

In 1950, China had a population of 600

million. Today it has over 1 billion.

When the United States started as an independent republic in the 18th century, it was a nation of only 3 million. Today it is over 200 million.

But life in these once undeveloped and agrarian countries is so much better than what it was 50 years ago; and certainly better than the life presently led by a mere 55 million Filipinos.

Simple sense dictates that we look to a more realistic, and honest, explanation for mass poverty than that offered by the distinguished Mr. Salas and the over-populationists.

The second theory is that the condition of the masses is explained primarily by bad government. The battle cry of this theory is that good government is the answer to the nation's problems. Elect one who is honest, and preferably prestigious, and we have solved the problems of the country, even if all he does is disseminate birth control devices and IRRI's high yielding varieties.

But a quick review of our politico-economic history easily shows that the moral explanation for mass poverty is as inaccurate and misleading as the population theory. The truth is that for the over-whelming part of this century, our governments have been run by upright men. It was only when Marcos took power in 1966, with the aid of upright men, that graft and corruption assumed scandalous proportions.

Before the war, the quality of our politics was synonymous with the qualities of Quezon and Osmena, Recto, Roxas, Osias, Yulo, Vargas, Sabido, Laurel, Alunan, Ventura and a host of illustrious others who stood as models of public rectitude.

But as early as that time, mass poverty had

already become the social problem, prompting Quezon to announce his program of social justice. Even when the country was still a possession of the United States in the 1930s, the head of the famed Sakdal movement, Benigno Ramos, was already moved to describe the Philippines as "*ang bayan ng mga pulubi at patay-gutom*" and the Filipino as "*makapantay na lamang ng hayop.*"

Adherents of the Statehood Movement should reflect on this.

Mass poverty in this country did not begin with political independence, or when the Philippines began to be run by Filipinos; and that poverty will not disappear simply be re-joining the American Union, which still has to resolve the poverty of its ethnic minorities. There are now 40 million impoverished Americans, representing 20% of their country's population.

Even in the good government years of the Commonwealth, mass poverty co-existed with decent and credible political leaderships, and we still have to see a more credible and dynamic leadership than the government of Quezon.

No one can say that at that time we were not a prayerful nation. We were already a nation which prayed; we have been praying for the last 400 years; and believed in miracles, but a nation also immersed in human suffering, tottering, as the historian Constantino reminds us, on the brink of a social upheaval which would be staved off only by the invasion of the Japanese Imperial Army.

After the war, on regaining independence, our governments continued to be dominated and managed by public servants who, basically, upheld the moral tradition of our pre-war politics. Although the issue of graft became the hallmark of post-war presidential contests, one must, in all objectivity and fairness, admit that corruption was kept at a tolerable level, and nowhere assumed the scale which came with the Marcos government.

Until Marcos, politics was a comparatively decent and morally respectable affair. One cannot look back to the administrations of former Presidents Roxas, Quirino, Magsaysay, Garcia and Macapagal without missing the basic decency which stamped their tenures.

But mass poverty was there. By 1966, when Marcos assumed office, terminating a long era of upright governments, the nation was in crisis, and poverty was more rampant than it had ever been.

It is obvious that we must look beyond the moral factor for the considerations that really explain the intractable persistence of the poverty problem.

The truth is that there has never been a necessary correlation between economic progress and political morality. The spectacular pace of industrial and economic development in the United States during the 19th century coincided with the rise of robber barons who bribed and corrupted politicians, and murdered their rivals, in a scale that makes the Marcos cronies look like a gang of pious incompetents.

There is as much monopoly and crony capitalism in South Korea as there was in the Philippines during Marcos, but one cannot begin to compare either the condition of the masses there with the condition of the masses here, or the economic performance of the two countries.

It is common knowledge that there is extensive corruption in the socialist bureaucracies, but socialist economies are thriving, and their people aren't plagued by mass unemployment, hunger and social insecurity.

Surprisingly, communists are without religion, moved by an ideology which negates God and prayers. But they are creating their own economic miracles, bent on making of earth an economic paradise, where human beings would live decently, and in dignity, where there would be no mendicancy and prostitution, and where the individual is conditioned to think in terms of the collective good as embodied in the state.

China and the Soviet Union are producing artists, scientists, medical and military technicians, and even basketball players, of superior quality and they are now deep in the age of nuclear power and space, creating the scientific basis for an even more dynamic future for their young.

This is not to denigrate the need for God, prayers, and credible leadership, but simply to stress the fact that mass poverty is fundamentally a function, or product, of factors that have nothing to do either with morals or religion, or even with what passes for credible leadership.

An entire people can pray intensely for the rest of their lives, work hard, have honest people in the government and yet remain immersed in misery.

And, corrolarily, a nation can, as in socialism, deny God, or, as in a capitalist country like the United States, produce robber barons and deceitful presidents, and still thrive and prosper materially.

This is a truth. An obvious truth which should not offend religious sensibilities.

But it should make church goers ponder.

What the poverty of the masses reflect: Underdevelopment and what it means.

Mass poverty is simply the reflection and necessary consequence of a deeper malignancy. That malignancy is neither overpopulation nor bad government.

It is economic underdevelopment.

What is economic underdevelopment?

Economic underdevelopment is a people's state of incapacity to produce their means of production: the machines and the tools that would enable them to produce goods, and to render services; the tools that produce needle and scissor the machines that produce engines; the mills that produce textiles; the equipments that produce typewriter and xerox machine.

What essentially distinguishes developed nations from the underdeveloped is that the former manufacture the means of production, while the latter do not; and because the latter do not, their capacity to generate wealth as well as employment is severely constricted; they are then rendered completely dependent on the industrial nations which, in turn, exploit that dependence.

Indonesia, which is abundantly endowed with natural resources, particularly wood and oil, is an example of an underdeveloped economy.

Japan, on the other hand, poorly endowed in natural resources, is an example of a highly developed economy.

But there is a vast world of difference between Indonesia and Japan.

Indonesia does not produce the heavy tools, the machineries, equipments and ocean vessels needed to extract oil underground, or with which to fell trees, haul them as logs to ports of shipment, transport them to markets overseas, and convert them to an infinite variety of finished products.

Without the drilling wells and machineries produced by Japan, Indonesia's forest and petroleum are useless even to itself.

This is the reason why Japan, a nation that is comparatively impoverished in natural resources, is a model of opulence, and can dictate the very terms of Indonesia's economic existence.

There is a saying that if you wish to keep a man from starving, it isn't enough that you give him fish. You must, better still, teach him how to fish.

There is a good deal of truth in that. But that truth isn't enough.

If you wish to keep a man from starving, you must not only teach him how to fish. Above all, you must teach him how to produce the fishing rod that would enable him to fish.

Otherwise, he remains an economic paraplegic, dependent on external factors for his survival.

Fish represents consumer goods. The fishing rod represents the means of production, or what is known In economic parlance as capital goods.

Every nation in the world that has an intelligent perception of its real interest aspires to be a nation capable not only of fishing, but of producing its own fishing rods, its own capital goods, its own means of production.

That is why they aspire to industrialize.

A nation that is producing its own means of production has an economy capable of generating employment opportunities to a limitless degree. Correspondingly, a nation that is incapable of producing the means of production has a very limited capacity to create wealth, and to employ people.

The Philippines, for example, has a textile industry. Employment is generated through the functioning of the textile factories. But employment stops there. We do not produce those factories. We import them.

In the case of Japan, it not only has a textile Industry. It has a capital goods industry that produces the machines used by the textile factories. That Is why the Japanese economy can employ incomparably more people than the Philippines. The Japanese economy creates employment, not only by operating textile mills, which we do, but, more importantly, by producing the machines needed by textile mills, which we do not do.

Every time our textile factories import spare parts and equipments from Japan, we create employment, not for Filipinos, but for the Japanese, and supply Japan with dollars, as we spend ours.

This is the reason why industrial economies, that is, economies capable of producing capital goods, have an inexhaustible capacity to create jobs. It has a self-sustaining dynamism. Consider the infinite and unceasing number of machines, and machine parts, tools and production instruments produced by industrial countries and you will realize why mass poverty does not afflict their societies.

On the other hand, an economy that does not produce its means of production, is lethargic, decadent and dependent.

An economy that is not industrialized has only the land to depend on with which to create wealth and employment. But land is limited. One cannot manufacture land, as one would manufacture machines. One cannot work the land every day, unlike factories which can be worked not only every day, but 24 hours every day.

Hence, land-based economies are economies that can never cope with the demand of a large, and expanding population for work opportunities. Land-based economies, particularly those with extensive populations, are invariably .plagued with mass poverty.

Like Africa and the Philippines.

In the very structure of our economy lies the fundamental explanation for our mass poverty. Until the structure is changed through the emergence and development of a dynamic industrial base, the masses cannot hope to be relieved of their misery. Not even the massive application of palliatives will relieve them of that misery. They have been the recipient of palliatives for the last 30 years. And they will continue to be miserable until this country finally moves from the pre-industrial to the industrial age.

The critical question:
Why the failure to industrialize?

Here we must ask the first critical question: Why then, unlike others, have we failed to move from the pre-industrial to the industrial age.

Our people have every right to ask this question because they are increasingly aware that once agrarian and impoverished economies in Asia - Japan, China, South Korea, India and Taiwan -

have already industrialized, and various more - Malaysia, Singapore, Pakistan - are near to being industrialized, and prospering because of that.

For this, we must first look to our economic system and the philosophy it embodies. A people's material condition, and the quality of their economy, are determined primarily by the economic order and philosophy which govern their lives.

---ooo---

II. The Intrinsic Limitations Of Capitalism As A System For Undertaking The Nation's Economic Transformation And Industrial Development

The nature of the economic system.

Our economic system is based on private capitalism. That system in turn is based on two precepts. One is that to private capital, or private enterprise, must be assigned the primary, if not exclusive, role of moving the economy.

The other is that private profit should, as it actually does, constitute the motivating force of economic activity.

Inherent in the system is a bias against the intervention and direct participation of the State, or public capital, in the development process. It is almost axiomatic to the private enterprise creed that the State should refrain from activism in the economy and must confine itself to the conventional categories of public service, such as maintaining peace and order, collecting taxes, enforcing the law, holding clean elections, constructing roads, bridges, ports and other infrastructure, known as social overheads, which facilitate the operations of private capital. The State's role in establishing industries should at most be indirect, such as giving private enterprise investment incentives and tax privileges.

An economic system which would limit to private capital the function of undertaking the radical transformation of the economy is almost automatically self-defeating. It is self-defeating for two reasons. One is that domestic private capital is hardly sufficient to meet the massive requirements of an industrial revolution. But the more important reason is that private capital is under no obligation, social or legal, to accomplish the economic transformation of the country.

If, for example, private capitalists do not find it personally gainful to invest in a particular industry, they will not do so, even if such an industry is absolutely essential for the industrialization of the country.

If private capital chooses to remain idle, or indulge in non-productive speculation, or lend itself at usurious interests, take flight abroad, or invest in prostitution dens, gambling casinos, race horses and fighting cocks, it is at full liberty to do so, even if an entire nation starves for want of industries and opportunities for productive employment

This is precisely the problem of the present government. President Aquino's repeated pleas for capitalists to start investing and get the economy moving are not meeting with response in spite of the credibility of her government. And there is no way to compel private capital to invest, much less invest in the direction needed by the economy.

In his critical description of private capitalism, Pope Paul VI said of it that it is:

> "a system which considers profit as the key motive for economic progress, competition as the supreme law of economics, and private ownership of the means of production as an absolute right that has no limits and carries no corresponding social obligation." (Populorum Progression)

There cannot be a higher social responsibility for private capital, in the context of the poverty problem, than to undertake the industrialization of the country. But it is not under a "corresponding social obligation to do so, " to use the papal phrase.

If the nation were to wait for private capital to launch an individual revolution, it might have to wait forever.

To begin with, today's Filipino capitalists, by and large, do not believe in industrialization, much less in full industrialization. One only has to review the policy and public statements of the nation's leading figures of capital, and their acknowledged ideologues, to be convinced of this point.

One reason for this is that the capitalist class here is composed, and dominated, largely by merchants, bankers, miners and plantation owners whose interests stand either to be inconvenienced or prejudiced by an industrialization program.

Such a program would entail, among others, allocating foreign exchange and domestic credit on the basis of priorities that would promote the program, and this could easily disrupt the freedom, prospects and opportunities of those who make their money importing and trading on luxuries, buying, selling and developing real estate, mining and exporting ores, speculating on securities and commodities, lending at usurious interests, and are otherwise engaged in activities, such as Duty-Free Tourist Shops, that are irrelevant to the requirements of industrialization.

But even within the tiny manufacturing sector itself, there are contradictions which impede it from assuming an expediting and effective role in the industrialization process.

The manufacturing sector is characterized by interdependence and inter-linkages. One industry requires for its raw materials items manufactured by other industries. For example, a manufacturer of food products requires tin cans produced by the tin can industry, or plastic bags produced by the plastic industry. The tin can and plastic industries in turn need materials produced by the metal and chemical industries, and so on.

The contradiction begins here. Many local industries prefer to patronize foreign suppliers rather than domestic producers. Members of the food industry for example, might prefer imported tin cans to tin cans produced locally. A reason usually advanced is that a required industrial input, such as steel, or tin cans, is generally cheaper if imported, particularly if tariffs on them are either reduced or abolished, as the IMF insists on.

But there are other reasons. Importing is one way of salting dollars; that is why many industries prefer to import their requirements rather than purchase these from local sources.

The following account, taken from a pre-martial law news item, concretely illustrates the contradiction within the manufacturing sector.

"Lack of interest on the put of certain manufacturing firms, particularly those run by aliens and former aliens who have become naturalized citizens, to tap locally available materials in their operations was viewed by a Filipino industrial executive yesterday as a factor that places a strange hold on the growth of local industries.

Ricardo P. Guevara, director of Mabuhay Vinyl Corporation, said such indifference could even be termed as "economic sabotage" when these firms would rather import such items to compete with locally produced materials and undermine the country's foreign exchange reserves.

And what makes the situation more sickening, Guevara pointed out, was that - in most cases-such importations were being made through under-pricing, dumping, and under-declaration of weight

Guevara cited the recent massive importations by certain alien manufacturers of polyvinyl chloride products who recently imported hundred of tons of PVC resins and compounds.

Guevara said he could not think of any justification for such an importation when these commodities are being produced locally out of the indigenous raw materials and in abundant quantity and quality comparable to the best imported ones." (Daily Mirror, August 11, 1967)

No less than a former chairman of the Board of Investments found it necessary to exhort members of big business to patronize and support the industries of their lesser colleagues.

"Industry Minister Vicente T. Paterno summoned big business to consider and follow government policy that takes note of the economics of sourcing from domestic suppliers existing within the peripherals of their productive facilities.

"Speaking before a group of prominent businessmen and industrialists who are members of the Philippine Business for Social Progress (PBSP) Paterno cited the manifold advantages of large-scale business interacting with its neighbors." (*Bulletin Today*. "Paterno Asks Increased Domestic Sourcing of Materials" June 11, 1979.)

The banking sector is another example. Banks want to charge as high as interest rates as possible because it profits them to do so. But this works havoc on the manufacturing sector.

Another problem is the mining sector. This sector objects to the establishment of the heavy industries that would enable the economy to convert its mineral ores to finished metal and metal products. Understandably so, because the industrialization of the economy would mean requiring the mining industry to sell a significant portion of what it mines to local smelting plants, instead of exporting these in the raw to the industrialized countries, like Japan. This would mean getting paid in pesos rather than in dollars, for one, and the end to quick and comparatively easy profits.

One doesn't hear of the mining sector urging the country's industrialization. Industrialization would work against its interest. Industrialization, for one, would lead to the banning of raw material exports.

We see that within the capitalist class, as well as within the manufacturing group within that class, there are deep and complex contradictions which impede it, as a class, from leading an industrial revolution.

There is no social conscience that compels members of that class to even help each other. This, one supposes, is among what Pope Paul VI meant.

The perceived failure, refusal and inability of domestic private capital to industrialize the economy has in turn led a school of development theoreticians to the curious idea that foreign private capital should then be enlisted for the task.

This, however, can only be counter-productive and overlooks the real interest of foreign investments in underdeveloped economies.

Why private foreign capitalism cannot develop an underdeveloped economy.

Private foreign capital, largely represented by transnational corporations, cannot possibly have an interest in seeing agricultural economies, which are markets for industrial products, transform into industrial economies. The reason is that there is a fundamental contradiction between the interest of transnational corporations, on one hand, and, on the other, the interest of underdeveloped economies striving towards development.

A Ford or General Motors, for example, would not want to see economies like the Philippines develop an independent car industry. An authentic Philippine car industry would certainly prejudice Ford and General Motors. The development of the car industry in South Korea and

Japan, once agrarian economies, have extensively injured the car industries of the United States and Europe, which had traditionally monopolized this line of production.

The same may be said of the damaging impact on the western economies of industries like textile, steel, shipbuilding, electronics, computers and watches, which the newly industrialized states of Asia have recently developed and which are now making inroads not only in foreign markets once dominated by western industries but in the very home markets of these industries themselves. The world is now witness to South Korea, Taiwanese and Japanese steel products, shoes, appliances, electronics, textiles, watches, etc. working havoc on American industries in the American market itself.

There is another major consideration which argues against a policy that relies on private foreign capital to undertake the industrialization of non-industrial economies.

An underdeveloped economy embarked on an industrial revolution must hasten its capital accumulation. This means that enterprises within the economy must continuously re-invest their surplus and profits in the economy.

Foreign private capital, however, is concerned with extracting, and shipping out as much of its profit from the host countries where it operates. That is why underdeveloped economies where foreign investments are heavily present find themselves perpetually short of capital. We have had foreign investments since the turn of the century, but this country has never taken off industrially, and continues to complain that it lacks capital.

The truth is that transnational corporations operating in non-industrial countries are concerned primarily with capturing these as markets for industrial products, which are shipped here in knocked-down parts, to be assembled by cheap domestic labor.

Once assembled into their completed forms, these products are then sold either in the domestic or export market.

It is not in the interest of transnational companies to develop the economies of non-industrial countries.

At most, the latter are to be developed as processing or assembly centers, which, because of their cheap and abundant labor, reduce the manufacturing cost of goods.

What passes off as the "manufacturing" and "industrial" operations of transnational corporations are but disguised export operations which transfer neither capital nor technology, and which veil a number of practices that enable these corporations to exploit the economy. Among these is the practice by which the mother company ships to its subsidiary (Ford US to Ford Philippines, for example) at an overprice, finished goods in unassembled form, which are then assembled by the subsidiary under the supervision of its foreign technicians, who are paid excessively. This is why transnational companies operating here cannot be expected to patronize or support local industries. They prefer, and are in fact compelled, to import their requirements from their head offices abroad.

As a result, the country is literally milked while preserved as a non-industrial economy performing what are essentially either processing or assembly-type operations that pass off as manufacturing activities. On top of this, transnational companies avail extensively of domestic credits, thereby reducing the amount of loan capital that would otherwise be channeled to local entrepreneurs.

The largest issuers of money market instruments, which are nothing more but uncollateralized promissory notes, are transnational companies.

> "Local borrowings of foreign companies operating here have remained unabated despite ceilings imposed by the government, SEC sources said yesterday." (Daily Express, May 10, 1980)

Private capitalism, Filipino and foreign, has had 100 years during which to industrialize the Philippines; but, judging by results, one must conclude that capitalism has failed dismally in this country and is manifestly inadequate to the requirements of an industrial revolution.

Capitalism in the Philippines has not even been able to establish a viable and self-sufficient tool industry. 85% of our hand tools are imported, and we import virtually all our machine tools.

India, on the other hand, can construct an entire nuclear reactor with local components, and has now broken into the age of space. South Korea and Taiwan have completed their first industrial revolution, and are on their way to a second. They now manufacture their own computers, blast furnaces, industrial plants, and even missiles, and have entered the age of high technology.

Local capitalism, in contrast, while displaying enormous sophistication in money market, financial, merchandising and other activities, cannot even produce a decent hammer.

Even the local baking industry complains that its technology is *"at least 100 years behind countries like Japan.* " (Business Times, "Bakers Deplore Outdated Equipment," May 30, 1983).

The fact is that we cannot even bake bread without imported equipments.

---ooo---

III.   Why Capitalism Succeeded Elsewhere In Generating An Industrial Revolution But Has Failed In The Philippines

The failure of capitalism to generate an industrial revolution in the Philippines raises a basic question. That is, why did capitalism lead to industrialism not only in the western world but also in Asia while failing so dismally in this country.

Elsewhere, the capitalist class is associated with the dynamic transformation of agrarian economies into industrial ones. The industrial revolution in Western Europe and the United States was a creation of capitalism. But in the Philippines, capitalism has produced nothing better than an impoverished agricultural economy, along with a class of shameless cronies.

The very condition of our economy is a searing indictment of the Filipino capitalist class whose counterparts abroad, not only in the West but also in the newly industrialized states of Latin America and Asia - Brazil, Mexico, India, South Korea, Taiwan and Singapore - have created miracles of economic transformation.

It is important that we understand why capitalism here has failed to produce an industrial revolution; why capitalism in the Philippines has failed to graduate from the pre-industrial to the industrial stage.

In the western world, where capitalism sired the industrial revolution, entrepreneurs functioned within the context of nation-states which were not only independent but which found it in their interest to promote and encourage industrialism as a national goal.

The opposite has been the case in the Philippines, and the reason for this will be explained in a latter part of this paper.

And so western governments promoted industrialism in the only way it could be promoted: by ensuring domestic industries control of the home market through an intensive program of protectionism. There was then no international economic policeman, like the IMF, which insisted that national economies should function on the basis of free trade, and that governments should refrain as much as possible from protecting national industries. Anti-protectionist thoughts, and formal espousal of free trade, came only with Adam Smith, who was never taken seriously, then and now, except by the IMF, and the Philippine government.

Turning to concrete examples, one might begin with England where the industrial revolution was born, and home to the free trade philosophy of Adam Smith.

From the beginning, the British government zealously protected its domestic industries. England was a colonial power and prohibited its colonies from engaging in industries that would compete with its domestic manufacturers. An illustration of this was how the British government liquidated the developed textile industry of India by cutting the thumbs of Indian weavers caught exercising their trade.

How the British government promoted British industries, particularly through conquest and colonialism, has been described in some detail by a noted political economist.

From her work, "*The Creation of World Poverty*" (Pluto Press Limited) Teresa Hayter informs us that:

> "As early as the seventeenth century when the British began enacting the Navigation Acts, colonies were prohibited by law from turning to any industry which might compete with the industry of the mother country. For example, the North American colonies were forbidden to manufacture caps, hats, woolen or iron goods.
>
> "One of the more notorious facts of British colonial history is that the British subsequently proceeded to destroy the industrial economy of India itself.
>
> "Once British industry was established, it was safe to argue the virtues of Free Trade." (Pp. 47,48, 51)

Next we might consider the case of Germany. Under Bismarck, who created that nation as a modem state, industrialization was made a national goal, and the protection of German industries official state policy. Originally an adherent of Free Trade, Bismarck turned to protectionism to make of Germany an industrial power.

Narrating Bismarck's shift from adherence to

Free Trade to his espousal of protectionism, the historian AJ.P. Taylor writes:

> "The changes in home and foreign affairs both sprang from Bismarck's abandonment of the liberal belief that all things would work together for good if only they were left alone. He ceased to believe that peace and prosperity were natural; he took thought for the morrow and secured them by conscious effort. Protection, as the name implied, involved the deliberate fostering of German industry and agriculture against the dictates of "economic law*." (A.J.P. Taylor, Bismarck 144, First Nel Mentor Edition,1968).
>
> "He studied political economy xxx and drafted all the principal tariffs. Having once abandoned Free Trade he now wanted thorough going protection, and stirred the sectional interests to bid against each other. The Conservative agrarians xxx agreed to the Tariff on iron and steel only in exchange for a high Tariff on grain." (Taylor, *Op. Cit.* 141)

By 1879, Protectionism, for both industry and agriculture, was firmly established in Germany, and thus did the modem German state begin.

That was 100 years after thirteen former colonies launched their industrial revolution in the American continent.

We turn to the United States.

The spectacular rise of industrialism in that once prairie country was preceded by its formal adoption of industrialization as a national objective, and of protectionism as the official policy for accomplishing that objective.

After its war of independence, the United States was faced with the choice either to preserve itself as an agricultural economy, which it was very much then, or to become, through deliberate policy, a manufacturing country like England.

The man responsible for steering that young republic away from its agricultural economy and for pushing it to the industrial age was Col. Alexander Hamilton, a military aide to Gen. Washington, who became America's first Secretary of the Treasury, and its first technocrat.

As America's first technocrat, Hamilton was asked by the U.S. House of Representatives to propose a developmental programme, which he did in his famous *Report on Manufacturers* in 1791.

In that report, Hamilton batted for a policy of protectionism, and repudiated the theory of Free Trade, on the ground that the United States, although preponderantly agricultural, should strive to be a powerful industrial state like England.

Free Trade would flood the American market with imported manufactures, particularly from England, and these would abort the birth of a domestic manufacturing capability, Hamilton argued.

And so he pleaded for a vigorous policy of protectionism which would preserve the home market for domestic industries.

The following passages from an extensive biography of Hamilton (Miller, Alexander *Hamilton and the Growth of a New Nation*, Harper Torchbooks) should be perused carefully by Philippine policy makers because they shed light on how America, as an agricultural country in the 18th century, resolved the issue between Agriculture and Industry, between Free Trade and Protectionism, which confronted it while still an underdeveloped economy, as these issues now confront us.

"Despite the progress made in manufacturing Hamilton considered the economy of the United States to be in a dangerous state of imbalance. The preponderance of agriculture impressed him as a source of weakness: by pursuing agriculture as single-mindedly as did Americans, Hamilton feared that they were perpetuating the very conditions from which they had sought to escape by declaring their independence - a colonial inferiority and dependence upon the more industrialized countries of Europe."

"Every country in the Old World sought to ensure a monopoly of its domestic markets for its own manufactures and to buy at little and to tell as much as possible abroad."

"Obviously, Hamilton was not likely to fall under the sway of the philosophy of laissez faire. For one thing, he was not persuaded, as were so many of his countrymen, that the freedom of the individual was best provided for by rigorously curtailing the powers of the state."

"Naturally, therefore, Hamilton concluded that free trade was a philosopher's version of the best of all possible worlds, not a picture of reality."

"It was time enough he added to think of free trade when the United States had firmly established its industries and attained with Great Britain a commanding position in world trade." (Pp. 284-292)

And the United States proceeded to become a great industrial power, so great that by the turn of the century, it was able to engage imperial Spain in naval battle, and annex the Philippines, on whom it would impose Free Trade.

In 1944, as the second world war drew to a close, the United States, then the undisputed industrial power in the world, organized the Bretton Woods Conference for the purpose of creating a new international economic order based on Free Trade, and established the IMF as the work) agency tasked with the mission of enforcing Free Trade rules.

But to turn back to Hamilton. Alter the young American republic had endorsed the strategic plan of its first technocrat, the U.S. government proceeded to enact tariff laws so prohibitive as to have provoked the agricultural South into thoughts of rebellion and secession.

Taussig, in his classic work on the history of American tariffs, tells us that in its effort to protect domestic manufacturers of steel rails from competition with England, the U.S. government imposed a duty on foreign steel rails equivalent to *"more than one hundred per cent on the foreign price."*

> "By 1877 the average price of steel rails in England was only a little over $31 per ton; and since 1877 the English price has not on the average been so high as $28 per ton. The duty of $28 which this country imposed therefore became equivalent to more than one hundred per cent on the foreign price." Taussig, *The Tariff History of the United States* p. 222, Capricorn Books).

The production of steel rails was a major stimulating factor in America's industrialization. It created a demand for steel, and provided a major support for the steel industry, deemed the mother of all industries.

As Taussig remarks, U.S. tariffs in a "vast number" of cases were actually prohibitive.

> "As everyone conversant with our tariff system knows, they were often excessive xxx. They were higher than was necessary to enable the domestic producers to hold their own. A vast number of duties were simply prohibitive." (p. 367)

American Tariff policy in the 18th- 19th centuries was expressive of the intense economic nationalism that transformed a prairie economy in the American continent into the foremost industrial power in the world.

How Asian countries industrialized,

Asia today prides itself in six countries, once agrarian economies, which transformed miraculously during this century. These countries prove that it is fully within the capabilities of Asians to create their own industrial revolution.

These are Japan, Singapore, India, China, Taiwan and South Korea.

Animated by different ideologies, these six non-Christian nations in Asia have been moved by different development strategies which, however, share one element in common: and that is, the direct and active role of the State in the economy, particularly as an industrial pioneer and entrepreneur.

The precedent was established by Japan during the Meiji regime. The Japanese government, impatient to industrialize, did not wait for a then timid private sector, and instead opted to pioneer and lead the industrial revolution.

The essence of the Japanese strategy was described in a classic text on the subject:

> "At the beginning of the Meiji period the merchant capitalists had no experience in managing modem industrial establishments and were shy of becoming entrepreneurs. The government itself therefore started enterprises in a number of fields. It built some of the railway lines and guaranteed the financial returns of others. There were government banks and insurance companies, as well as factories. The government set up a cotton spinning mill, a silk reeling mill, an agricultural machinery plant, a cement works, a glass factory, a brick factory, nine modem mines, and shipyards, as well as military installations." *(Maddison, Economic Growth in Japan and the USSR 22.23, Pitman Press 1969.)*

The pioneering role of the government, and the intensity of its commitment to industrialization, eventually contaminated the entire population.

> "As the nineteenth century drew to a close, Japan's business and political leaders were gripped by a fever of industrialization." (Lockwood, *The Economic Development of Japan* 16 Princeton University Press.)

As Lockwood further narrates, "experimental factories were set up to produce cement, sugar, beer, glass, chemicals and a variety of Western-type goods." (*Op. Cit.* 14)

In 1901 the country launched the government-owned Yawata Iron Works (Op. Cit.

24).

The concept that, in the context of Asian realities, the State must assume the initiative in engineering an industrial revolution, has become a tradition to which every government in Asia now adheres.

In *Singapore$_y$* which the western press points as a model of "free enterprise," the government owns and operates 450 state corporations functioning in spheres normally reserved for private enterprise. And this, in a city-state of only 3 million people.

The following dispatch from the Agence France Press is highly revealing, and completely shatters the myth that Singapore is an economy based on "free and private enterprise."

> "Singapore, Dec. 30 (AFP) - Local business representatives urged the government of Singapore to stop competing with them.
> Subsidiaries and associated companies together have entered almost every facet of business dealings in Singapore." (Bulletin Today, *"Singapore Government asked to stop competing with private business."* p. 14)

And from a work on the subject, we learn about the role of government:

> "Apart from supplying the infrastructure, the Government had to involve itself in direct ownership and control of many industrial, financial and commercial enterprises. Some of these constituted risk-taking ventures in partnership with the private sector, in the early years when investors needed encouragement." *(Socialism That Works, The Singapore Way* p.

83, Federal Publications, Singapore)

India, guided by the socialist vision of Nehru, adopted industrialization as a national goal from the moment it acquired its independence in 1949. It based its development strategy on the principle that industrialism is to be an affair principally between the State and Indian industrialists with foreign investments given a secondary role. It now ranks as the ninth industrial power.

This explains the pervasive presence in the Indian economy of the government which functions alongside the private sector, and the elaborate structure of import and foreign exchange controls designed to preserve the home market for Indian industries by prohibiting and/or severely restricting the imports of foreign goods, particularly those already produced by local industries. The Indian government is in virtually every major industry, from steel to oil and banking.

China, of course, undertook her industrial revolution through the socialist path, with the State playing not only a leading and major role, as in India, but as the dominant factor in the economy, with all major means of production reserved exclusively for it.

In *Taiwan and South Korea* government elaborately protects domestic industries from import competition and directly owns and operates numerous industries, either entirely or in partnership with private capital.

A Congressional task force sent by the U.S. Congress to study the trade situation in Asia reported the intense import restrictions by the "new Japans" namely, Taiwan and South Korea.

"NEW YORK, Feb. 15 (UPI) - A US congressional task force says the type of trade crisis the United States has experienced with Japan could recur with "new Japans" of the Far East like Taiwan and South Korea - and later other developing nations throughout the world.

Regarding Taiwan and South Korea the report says:

The two nations impose numerous import restrictions on US and other nations goods on the grounds that they are developing economies. Yet they have to a large extent graduated into the ranks of the developed economies and special protection is no longer justifiable." (*Bulletin Today*, US Warns of Rising Asian Imports, Feb. 16, 1979)

As for the role of the state in Taiwan, the following observation made by a local reporter should be of interest to those who think of Taiwan as a "free enterprise" economy.

"Private enterprises are encouraged but only to the extent where private economic benefit does not interfere with that of the state. The Taiwan state played a big role in stimulating industry; first, through 10 major construction projects, and now through the newly conceived 12 projects." (*Daily Express*, June 17, 1983, "Taiwan Development Plans" by E.P.Romualdez)

Philippine policy towards industrialism has followed a course completely the opposite of what the western world and developed Asian states have taken.

Here, national policy has been actually

hostile towards industrialization, particularly when coupled with proposals for protecting domestic industries. In addition, there is a built-in prejudice against the State performing a direct and active role in the economy.

In the Philippines industrialization and protectionism have been espoused and applied as official policies of State only for a fleeting period of 12 years out of the 40 years that we have been in existence as a republic. That was during the period 1950-1961 when, because of a foreign exchange crisis in 1949, we were forced to institute controls on imports and foreign exchange transactions. But those were completely dismantled in 1962 on pressure of the IMF and the U.S. which tantalized us with a $300 million loan.

India has been undeviatingly protectionist since her independence in 1949, or a total of 37 years; South Korea since the 1960s, or a total of 25 years; Taiwan, since the 1950s, or a total of 36 years; China, since the communist take-over in 1949, or a total of 37 years; and Japan, the industrial colossus, since the 1900s, or a total of almost 90 years.

In this closing decade of the 20th century, Philippine policy continues opposed to heavy industries, avoids talks of industrialization and protectionism, persists in preserving agriculture as the centerpiece of development. In talking of industries our policy makers carefully limit their meaning to "small and medium" enterprises, using labor-intensive techniques, like slipper making, furniture, garments, and bakeries.

It is as if we were determined, as a matter of policy, to remain underdeveloped, backward and poor; and no one can deny that, alone in Asia, we have so far succeeded brilliantly in that resolve.

We must cure ourselves of that perversity, as a man would of a suicidal tendency. And so, it is important that we trace the roots of that perversion and madness by probing into the recesses of our national past.

It is a past dominated and shaped by the unhealthy dynamics of our international relations; more particularly, by what has been described as Philippine-American special relations.

That relation is deemed "special" because unlike any relation, it has been the central and controlling influence in our internal affairs. It accounts for the psychosis so disturbingly reflected in the hostility of our policies against industrialization; a hostility which has arrested our own development.

We are a 40-year adult who refuses to grow up, driven by an infantile sense of dependence on a mother who has made it a point to preserve that sense of dependence, by blandishments preferably, but by force, if necessary.

That is the central lesson of Martial Law, as we shall see. And we must understand the real meaning of that experience if we are to write a meaningful constitution. For martial law was this nation's most important experience since independence, and to a large extent a new constitution must draw from the lessons of that experience, properly interpreted. But to understand its real meaning we must look back 90 years ago when the U.S. government, abandoning all commitments to human rights, human equality and democracy, launched its own imperialism in Asia, interrupted our war of independence, and annexed us against our will, for the most sordid of commercial reasons.

To that fateful event may be traced the modern origin of mass poverty in the Philippines, and the eventual rise of the Marcos dictatorship.

---oOo---

IV. The Failure Of Philippine Capitalism To Generate An Industrial Revolution Traceable Directly To The Colonial Nature Of Philippine-American Relations

The tradition of Free Trade and anti-industrialism, which so strongly dominates Philippine policy, dates to the formulation in the U.S. Senate of the reasons for the annexation and colonization of this country.

In January 4, 1900, Senator Albert J. Beveridge introduced a resolution which established permanent United States sovereignty in the Philippines.

In defense of that resolution, which committed the United States to a career of imperialism in Southeast Asia, Beveridge asserted in the floor of the Senate:

> "The Philippines are ours forever... And just beyond the Philippines are China's illimitable markets. We will not retreat from either.
>
> "Our largest trade henceforth must be with Asia. The Pacific is our ocean. More and more Europe will manufacture the most it

consumes. Where shall we turn for consumers of our surplus. Geography answers the question. China is our natural customer. .. The Philippines give us a base at the door of all the East."

Two years earlier, in a speech titled "*The March of the Flag,*" Beveridge had spelled out with more specificity his vision of Philippine-American relations. He said then:

"The riches of the Philippine have hardly been touched by the finger tips of modern methods. And they produce what we consume, and consume what we produce - the very predestination of reciprocity - a reciprocity not made with hands, eternal in the heavens."

"They sell hemp, sugar, coconuts, fruits of the tropics, timbers of price like mahogany; they buy flour, clothing, tools implements, machinery and all that we can raise and make. Their trade will be ours in time." (Reproduced in Boorstin, "*An American Primer,*" New American Library 1966)

The implementation of the colonialist vision, so vigorously asserted by Beveridge, required that a free trading relationship between the Philippines and the United States be established. If the Philippines is to function as a market for America's manufactured goods, and as a supplier of agricultural products, then our Government should be inhibited from taking any steps that would in any way restrict or discourage the flow of goods from the United States. Our sovereign right to protect our domestic market and domestic industries from unwarranted imports should be immobilized. That is the only way an agricultural country can be preserved agricultural, and hindered from developing a manufacturing capability.

It was from this colonialist premise that American economic policy towards the Philippines was forged; and since that premise, as we shall see, has not changed since it was first formulated by Beveridge in 1900, the policy would persist even to this date, long after the Philippines had, theoretically, ceased to be an American colony.

To understand why the colonialist vision, which constitutes the vital premise of American policy in the Philippines, persists to this day, one must look to an even more revealing passage in Beveridge's "*The March of the Flag*" speech.

That speech ominously foreshadowed the design of the United States for Asia in the years ahead. Asia's doors, asserted Beveridge, "*must not be shut against American trade.*" And he predicted that "*Within five decades the bulk of Oriental commerce will be ours.*"

> "So Hawaii furnish us a naval base in the heart of the Pacific xxx Manila another, at the gates of Asia - Asia, to the trade of whose hundreds of millions American merchants, manufacturers, farmers, have as good right as those of Germany or France, or Russia or England; xxx Asia, whose doors must not be shut against American trade. Within five decades the bulk of Oriental commerce will be ours."

As early as that time one could already foretell what American policy towards the Philippines would be, for the rest of this century, if not for all time: to force and preserve open the Philippine market as widely as possible to

American exports; a policy which, since 1962, when the Decontrol Program took effect, has been enforced through the loan conditionalities of the IMF.

The global interest of the U.S. today require more than ever that the Philippines be retained as an economic colony. Hounded by surpluses in both her manufacturing and agricultural sectors, the U.S. has found it absolutely imperative to open not only the markets of Asia but the rest of the world to her exports. And we are about the only country in Asia, if not in the world, that has been willing to submit to America's imperial requirements as a matter of routine.

Summarized hereunder are the events which have implanted Free Trade in the very interstices of Philippine policy since 1909, when it was first legislated on us by the U.S. Congress.

1.   The Payne-Aldrich Law of 1909.- Under this law, which the U.S. Congress enacted in 1909, Free Trade was made the basis of Philippine-American economic relations. Our government was literally deprived of the right to limit and discourage importations from the U.S., either directly, such as through import quotas, or indirectly, such as through tariffs. This was passed over the objections of our Philippine Assembly.

In 1941, after 32 long years of Free Trade, the Philippines was dragged into the US-Japanese war. We were assaulted and invaded by an Asian country which, at the turn of the century, was, like us, a feudal and agricultural economy.

But by 1941, Japan's extreme

protectionism and nationalism had resulted in a powerful industrial machinery that could supply all the logistical requirements of an invading army, from shoes to guns, tanks, battleships and aircrafts.

The Philippines could not even produce a toy gun. We didn't have a toy industry. We simply imported toys from Japan.

President Quezon during the Commonwealth had attempted to industrialize the economy: but Free Trade, which inhibited our government from protecting domestic industries and from restraining imports, made his efforts an exercise in total futility.

U.S. colonial policy had succeeded in doing to us what the British attempted, unsuccessfully, to do to her in the 18th century.

2.   The Bell Trade Act of 1946. - This was the law enacted by the U.S Congress on the eve of our independence. It required the Philippines to continue and extend, for a specified period beyond independence, the Free Trade relation in exchange for post-war financial and economic assistance from the U.S. government. The late Claro M. Recto described this law as the basis of America's post-war "anti-industrialization policy in the Philippines. " We were literally coerced into accepting the Bell Act by the devastated condition of our economy after the war.

In arguing against the Free Trade provision of the Bell Act, the late Salvador Araneta, easily the most far seeing political economist of his generation, argued strenuously that the Act would condemn the Philippines to a "colonial economy."

"If in 1909 our leaden were justified in opposing Free Trade, after past experience, we should with greater reason object to it today. "The Bell Act equals a colonial economy." (see Araneta, Economic Reexamination of the Philippines. 101, 135).

And Claro M. Recto, describing how the Bell Act was forced on the Filipino people, bitterly recalled that:

"Our country was in ruins, the national economy was completely dislocated, there was no food, nor shelter, nor clothing, for our people as a result of the war. Considering our state of economic distress xxx the proponents of the Trade Agreement wielded a formidable weapon over our people." (Recto, *Our Trade Relations with the United States* speech delivered at the Commencement Exercises of the University of the East, April 4, 1954).

3. *The Decontrol Program of1962.* - In 1962, in exchange for a stabilization loan of $300 Million from the U.S. and the IMF-WB Group, we submitted to a program which, among others, required us to adhere to the IMF charter prohibiting the application of controls on imports and fell foreign exchange transactions. Under the program we were required to eliminate the system of import and foreign exchange controls which had been in force during the period 1950-1961. We had been compelled to avail of import controls then because of a foreign exchange crisis in 1949. That crisis was a direct result of the Free Trade provision in the 1946 Bell Trade Act.

If the 1909 Payne-Aldrich law introduced Philippine policy to Free Trade, the *1962 decontrol program not only reiterated Philippine commitment to a policy of unrestricted importations but also marked the beginning of the IMF's direct involvement in our policy processes, and the rise of a Filipino technocratic class which would defend and speak for IMF-sponsored programmes.* That program also started our foreign debt problem.

In 1962, our foreign debt stood only at $150 million. Three years after Decontrol, it had risen to $600 million, or by four times.

Today that debt stands at $26 Billion.

4. *The 1970 Devaluation and adoption of the floating rate.* - In 1969, a foreign exchange crisis forced the Philippines to apply for the usual stabilized loan; and, as usual, the IMF insisted on conditions that forced our government to reaffirm Philippine commitment, made in 1962, to an import policy basically free from direct controls and restrictions. This time, that commitment came in the form of an agreement to "float" the peso, and allow it to seek its dollar value on the basis of market forces; that is, the supply and demand for dollars.

The concept of the "floating rate" requires a government adopting it to refrain from interfering with the free market for foreign exchange; meaning, that it should abstain from directly placing limits on imports on the theory that such limits would not enable the currency (Peso) to find its true value on the basis of market forces working freely.

The floating rate was a device conceived to provide the IMF a continuing pretext for urging on its members a foreign exchange and import system unencumbered by restrictions, as dictated by the charter of that organization. In addition, the floating system virtually ensured the continuous devaluation of the currency, a standard prescription of the IMF to stimulate exports, *and for making it progressively cheaper for foreign investments to buy into the economy.* We committed ourselves to the floating system in 1970 in exchange for a stabilization loan. At the time, the pesos's fixed official rate was P3.90:$1. When it was floated, the peso's value sunk to P5.50:$1, and from thereon progressively sunk to its present level of P20.50:$1.

It was argued by Messers. Virata and company that floating the peso would be good for the country's international reserves. At the time the peso was floated in 1970, the foreign debt stood at only a little over $1 Billion. Over a period of 16 years, it expanded twenty-six times. And we have literally nothing to show for it in terms of basic industries.

5. *The Labor-Intensive, Export-Oriented development strategy of the Martial Law Government.* - In September 1972, martial law was declared on the ground, among others, that the economy was in deep crisis. Despite the floating of the peso in 1970, which the IMF claimed would improve the foreign exchange situation, the international reserve position of the country had deteriorated, and a $1 Billion debt in that year had swelled to $1.9

Billion in two years time.

The declaration of martial law was swiftly followed by the adoption of a development strategy described *"labor-intensive and export-oriented."*

This meant the following: (1) because the program is export-oriented, the country must continue floating the peso because the float was the only way the peso could achieve a "realistic foreign exchange rate," and such a "realistic foreign exchange rate," in turn, is necessary to stimulate exports; (2) the country is to refrain from engaging in industries that are capital-intensive, and should instead concentrate on labor-intensive industries that are export-oriented.

The program, in brief, explicitly committed the Philippines against heavy industries which constitute the essence of industrialization; to continue adhering to an import and foreign exchange policy free from restrictions, that is, Free Trade; and to utilize devaluation as the principal instrument for rectifying imbalances in the country's international trade.

6. *Accession to and Membership in GATT.* - In addition to adopting the export-oriented, labor-intensive development program, the country, led by Mr. Virata, broke a long standing Philippine tradition against membership in GATT. In 1975, the Philippines finally joined that international body. Members of that organization commit to dismantle their tariffs. From then on, we would progressively dismantle tariffs, in addition to refraining from direct import control measures. This meant a commitment to total and absolute Free Trade, more total and absolute even than that contemplated by the IMF, which prohibits direct controls on imports and foreign currency transactions, but allows tarrifs.

For example, the United States and Japan are members of GATT and as such are committed to the elimination of tariffs. But both ignore IMF requirements for an import policy free from restrictions. Both the U.S and Japan continue protecting their domestic industries mainly through actions which directly limit imports, such as outright bans, import quotas and controls on foreign exchange transactions openly violative of IMFs Free Trade rules.

7. *Virata's 1976 Utter of Commitment to the IMF pledging that the government will refrain from the use of import and foreign exchange controls as a means of protecting domestic industries.* - As if all prior commitments were not enough to ensure an anti-protectionist program, Mr. Virata in 1976 wrote the Managing Director of the IMF explicitly pledging that the Philippine government will refrain from and avoid a policy that utilizes import and foreign exchange controls as a means of protecting domestic industries. The pertinent text of Mr. Virata's letter is reproduced hereunder:

"Looking ahead it is our intention to substantially phase out the use of exchange restrictions *especially those which are maintained for industrial protection.* This will be coordinated with the Department of Industry's policy in regard to the reduction in tarrif protection. *We intend to accelerate in*

1976 the transfer of selected items to the freely importable list xxx " (Utter of Finance Secretary Cesar Virata to Mr. H. Johannes Witteveen, Managing Director of IMF. March 5. 1976)

In the long era of free trade spanned by the 1909 Payne-Aldrich Law and the 1946 Bell Trade Act, and in the long line of commitments to a policy of unrestricted imports which our government has made since 1962, may be found the main explanation for this country's primitive, pre-industrial economy and the resulting mass poverty.

U.S. policy since 1909 has brilliantly made good the pledge of Senator Beveridge that the Philippines shall import manufactured goods from the United States, and supply the latter with agricultural produce. The U.S. has accomplished this by coercing and maneuvering the country into commitments under which our government was rendered powerless, or made to agree that it would render itself powerless, to protect our domestic industries and international reserves from the unrestrained invasion of foreign goods, even in the face of bankruptcy.

This is the meaning of the import liberalization program.

If capitalism in the Philippines has failed to evolve into industrial capitalism, it is because the course of its own development had been dictated and predetermined from the start by American colonial policy which decreed that the Philippines shall not develop industrially.

Hence, unlike its counterparts elsewhere, capitalism in the Philippines was never able to perform the revolutionary role of transforming an agrarian economy into an industrial one. Capitalists here do not even seem to have heard of the industrial revolution, which explains the alliance of many of them with colonialist forces bent on freezing our economy in its pre-industrial mold.

That is why in the business community Marcos and the U.S. found many ready supporters for martial law and its policies.

We now turn to that dark episode in our history, and it is important that we grasp its essential meaning.

---ooo---

V. The Real Meaning Of Martial Law: How The U.S. Government Encouraged And Utilized The Marcos Dictatorship And Its Technocrats To Overcome A National Policy Established By Congress In 1969 To Industrialize The Economy And Abandon Free Trade, As Well As To Suppress An Established Trend In The 1971 Constitutional Convention Towards A Constitution That Would Have Made Industrialization And Protectionism Matters Of State Policy.

Martial law was something much more than just the ambition of one man to be dictator for life. It was the dynamics of Philippine-American relations violently reacting to two distinct political events that had spelled the death of Free Trade rule and IMF programmes in the Philippines.

The first of that event was the passage of House Joint Resolution No. 2 in 1969, otherwise known as the Magna Carta of Social Justice and Economic Freedom.

1969 House Joint Resolution No. 2 of the Philippine Congress.

In 1969, engulfed by the crisis rooted in the 1962 IMF decontrol programme, and in the face of Mr.Marcos' decision to persist with that programme despite the crisis, the Philippine Congress staged an open rebellion, and in a historic, unprecedented moment in Philippine political history, enacted, at a special session called for the purpose, a joint resolution demanding that the nation pursue a program of industrialization, abandon Free Trade, turn to protectionism, repudiate Free Enterprise, and institute a program of economic Filipinization and social justice.

Popular support for that document was so overwhelming as to have compelled Marcos to sign it into law on August 4, 1969, 3 months before the presidential elections of that year.

The *Magna Carta* was sponsored in the House of Representatives by then Speaker Jose B. Laurel, Jr., who had initiated the entire movement, and was steered in the Senate by former Jose W. Diokno, then chairman of the influential Senate Committee on Economic affairs which, at an earlier date had successfully pressed for the regulation of the entire oil industry.

In his sponsorship speech, Laurel, Jr., invoked the very same arguments voiced decades earlier by the nationalists who had opposed the 1909 Free Trade legislation and the Bell Trade Act of 1946; and, like others before him, pointed to a non-industrial, agricultural economy as the reason for the nation's massive poverty.

> "Many of our social problems stem from an archaic economic structure that is unable to meet the employment requirements of 37 million people, growing at the rate of almost 3.33b a year. It is an economic structure marked by the conspicuous absence of significant manufacturing capabilities and dependent mainly on agricultural pursuits is the largest source of the country's income and employment opportunities.
>
> "Only by industrializing the economy through the establishment of basic industries, particularly those that will utilize indigenous raw materials can we hope to resolve the perennial problem of mass unemployment and marginal incomes that hound the lives of our people."

That was in 1969, when the nation had only 37 million for its population.

To implement an industrialization program, Laurel, alluding to one of the principles of the Magna Carta, called for a policy of protectionism.

> "If we are to induce Filipino capitalists to invest in desirable industries, we must assure their products of an effective and controlling share of the domestic market. All other considerations are secondary.
>
> "And we can assure our entrepreneurs

control over the domestic market for their products only if they are effectively protected against foreign imports. This is the primary purpose of tariffs and of import and foreign exchange restrictions."

House Joint Resolution No. 2, Laurel in effect was saying, called for the abandonment of the Decontrol Program which had been in force since 1962. The message could not have been clearer.

But the Magna Carta went beyond that. As Laurel proceeded to inform his colleagues in the House:

"The Resolution proposes an effective government development institution that will vigorously push through a program of industrial *pioneering.*"

The signing of that historic resolution into law by then President Marcos on August 4, 1969 meant that the country had finally broken the spell of Free Trade and, with it, the IMF programme.

By that Resolution, our people made clear that they were opting for the kind of development strategy worked out by other industrialized states in Asia.

But the Magna Carta would, a year later, be rendered dead law by the floating rate.

Colonialist countermoves.

The forces of Free Trade, led in the Philippines by Virata, made their countermove.

When the Philippine government applied for a stabilization loan in late 1969, the IMF required it to adopt the system of floating rate.

As discussed earlier, the floating rate was a system designed to determine the peso's dollar value solely on the basis of market forces. Under the system, the peso would be unhinged from its fixed official rate (at that time P3.90:$1), and allowed to float in order to seek, in technocratic parlance, a "realistic foreign exchange rate."

Its value would then be established every day in accordance with the supply of and demand for dollars.

The system automatically committed our government to refrain from intervening in import and foreign exchange transactions on the theory that such intervention would disturb the free workings of market forces.

There would have been no point in the government floating the peso in order to allow its value to be established by market forces if it would control imports and other transactions involving foreign exchange. Such control would interfere with the free operation of market forces.

In brief, the floating rate committed our government to a policy completely opposed to the directives of the Magna Carta which had called for direct controls on imports and other transactions involving foreign exchange as a means of protecting and encouraging local industries.

That was how the IMF-WB Group, working with the Marcos technocrats, undermined and defied the directives of House Joint Resolution No. 2.

Effect of the floating rate.

The impact of the floating rate on the

economy was swift and traumatic. The almost 50% devaluation to which it led produced an inflation rate that ranked third among IMF member countries, surpassing even the inflation rate in war torn Vietnam.

Based on a report of the Congressional Economic Planning Office, Laurel, Jr., made the following assessment of the consequences of the floating system:

> "Since the suit of the floating rate system, the local manufacturing sector has not been able to prosecute plans for expansion. In not a few cases, industries could not even maintain their old production levels.
>
> "That the floating rate system is inconsistent with effective industrial planning is demonstrated in the current Four-Year Development Program. Capital requirements have been projected under the assumption that no further deterioration in the exchange rate shall take place during the implementation of the program.
>
> It cannot be overemphasized that an exchange rate which is subject to day-to-day fluctuations does not augur well for industrial advancement. In order to have a concrete basis for future planning, the exchange rate must be fixed. Then and only then can our industries embark on well-planned operations." (Laurel, *Report on the National Economy 29*, Lyceum Press, Inc.)

But the floating system was precisely intended to make industrial planning impossible. It was an integral part of the Free Trade mechanism and the strategy to suppress industrialization.

The floating rate notwithstanding, the fact

remained, however, that by 1969 the issues had been joined. Free Trade and anti-industrialism had been repudiated by the Filipino people officially through Congress in 1969, and that repudiation would, two years later, be reiterated in a higher and more strategic forum: in the 1971 Constitutional Convention, before martial law was declared.

This was the second political event to which colonialist forces reacted, compelling them eventually to declare martial law.

The 1971 Constitutional Convention.

The policies advocated by Congress in its Magna Carta of 1969 were not only affirmed, but considerably strengthened by the then ongoing Constitutional Convention, which assembled in 1971.

The public had clamored for such a Convention because of the widespread feeling that nothing less than the overhaul of the old constitution could possibly lead to much needed social and economic changes.

The Convention evolved into an instrument of the nationalist struggle, and by mid-1972 its organic committees had completed their reports which embodied a host of constitutional proposals which disturbed, and could only have panicked, the foreign business community, as well as the U.S. government and the IMF.

One of the major lobby groups of foreign interests was the Philippine Association. In December 1971, that body circulated its members with a newsletter expressing concern over what it described as the *"ultra-nationalistic" and "socialist"* trend in the Convention.

"Con-Con Direction"
"There is a strong move toward nationalization and socialism in the Convention with disturbing implications for the local as well as foreign business community."

The circular referred specifically to the following particular proposal sponsored by a number of Convention committees:

"The State shall undertake an integrated, nationalistic and socially oriented economic plan that shall efficiently promote rapid industrialization xxx (Sponsored by the Committee on Industrialization, Committee on Budget and Appropriation, Committee on Natural Resources, Committee on Trade, Tariff and Commerce, Committee on Science and Technology)."

The Convention was calling not only for industrialization but for "rapid industrialization."

The Far Eastern Economic Review in its issue of January 15, 1972, reporting on developments in the Convention observed that:

"It is, in fact, only in the economic field that one can see a clearcut pattern - and a clearcut break with the past - beginning to emerge.
"xxx the principle of economic nationalism has gained sufficient currency here to vitually ensure its enshrinement in the constitution." (Sterner, "Instant Revolution," p. 20)

The Convention was in fact going far beyond

the policies decreed two years earlier by House Joint Resolution No. 2, which the Marcos government and the IMF had ignored. If the powerful trend towards protectionism, industrialism and economic nationalism was to be reversed at all, there was only one course open to the forces of Free Trade. And that was martial law.

Had the Convention succeeded in finalizing into a finished constitution the proposals contained in its organic committee reports, as it was on its way to doing, there would have been no way for the colonialists to continue with Free Trade and the IMF programmes in the Philippines. They could not have defied the new constitution that was then emerging the way they defied House Joint Resolution No. 2 passed by Congress two years earlier.

And so, martial law was declared, to save Marcos, as well as the colonialist vision of Senator Beveridge.

With martial law, the anti-imperialist trend in the convention was aborted, and a colonial constitution enacted.

Martial law and the consolidation of colonialist forces working through the technocrats.

Martial law completely reversed the unmistakable will of the Filipino people, as expressed in House Joint Resolution No. 2 and in the organic committee reports of the Constitutional Convention.

Immediately upon declaration of martial law, the Board of Investments, led by then Minister Vicente Paterno, removed heavy industries from the priority list of the government's investment programme on the ground that the thrust of the martial law government would be on labor-intensive projects.

In its issue of January 28, 1973, four months after martial law had been declared, the Times Journal carried this revealing story:

> "Total of 23 industry areas led by steel manufacturing and the proposed PI Billion petrochemical complex, have been proposed for deletion from the Fifth Investment Priorities Plan by the Board of Investments.
>
> xxx
>
> "The deletions are being made partly in view of the Government's current emphasis on Labor-intensive projects to ease the country's unemployment situation.
>
> "The BOI recently passed a resolution calling for strict application of labor intensive criterion in the selection of projects to be included in the Investment Priorities Plan (IPP)." (*The Times Journal.* "23 Industry Areas Proposed To Be Scrapped from Investment Program," January 22, 1973 p. 5, Business Journal section.)

The BOI lost no time dismantling the directives of Congress in 1969 for a program of real industrialization.

In that resolution of the BOI was fully expressed the anti-industrialization program of martial law; a program that openly defied the people's will as expressed in the 1969 *Magna Carta.*

Finance Minister Virata immediately pushed, successfully, for Philippine accession to, and membership in, GATT, breaking a long standing policy against membership in that body, which is charged with the task of eliminating tariffs. That pledged our government to a program of tariff elimination.

And NEDA Chairman Sicat, joined by then Labor Minister Bias Ople and Executive Secretary Alejandro Melchor, pressed for the "labor-intensive, export-oriented" development plan.

As discussed earlier, the purpose of the labor-intensive, export-oriented programme was to commit the government to a policy: (1) against heavy industrialization, and (2) which confines industrial development to projects whose productivity depends mainly on labor power rather than machine power, thus dictating a correspondingly low level of industrial technology.

That is why it is called "labor-intensive," as distinguished from "capital intensive." By this, a nation's industrial development would be kept minimal and rudimentary.

Ironically, at the time that the BOI was de-listing capital intensive industries from the government's priorities. South Korea was starting its program of heavy industries, to be led by an integrated steel plant, which it established in defiance of IMF-WB recommendations.

An integral part of the "labor-intensive, export-oriented" programme was the floating rate which ensured the progressive devaluation of the peso as a means of encouraging exports.

Actually, devaluation is an expedient to make it progressively cheaper for foreign capital to buy into the Philippine economy.

Equally integral to the programme was a policy of cheap labor, because this was a way of making the products of labor-intensive industries attractive in the world market.

The strategy, in brief, was an outright assault against industrialization and labor. (1) to prevent industrialization, which had been declared a national objective by Congress in 1969, and (2) to make labor as cheap a commodity as possible for foreign investments. Such was the cornerstone and essence of martial law economics as espoused, intellectualized and implemented by Messrs. Sicat, Virata, Ople, Melchor and Paterno, the five technocrats who, with the IMF, were most responsible for propagandizing the program, and urging its national acceptance.

The programme could never have been mounted in the Philippines had we remained a democracy. In feet, as a democracy, we would have been launched on an industrial revolution, based on the program of policies formulated by Congress in 1969, and approved by Malacanang, as well as the emerging constitution, before martial law was declared.

Martial law had to be declared for the reason, among others, that the multinational companies had to be induced into the country.

Paterno would explain this in utmost candor:

> "The country needed martial law to take the steps to attract foreign investments" according to Vicente T. Paterno, chairman of the Board of Investments.
>
> "Paterno explained in a speech before the recent regional seminar of the Asian-American Free Labor Institute that "some of our businessmen still oppose participation of foreign capital in labor intensive export enterprises in the desire to avoid competition from the foreign investor." (Bulletin Today, "Martial Law Needed By Economy - Paterno"

April 19, 1973.)

In those remarks of Paterno are embodied not only the political and economic crime of the technocracy which he represented, but the heavy arrogance and the mindless inhumanity which characterized the technocratic tenure during that long night of martial law.

TO VIRATA, PATERNO, MELCHOR, OPLE, SICAT, ET AL., IT DID NOT MATTER THAT THE NATIONAL WILL AS EXPRESSED IN THE 1969 MAGNA CARTA, HAD BEEN DEFIED; THAT DEMOCRACY HAD BEEN EXTIN-GUISHED; THAT THOUSANDS LANGUISHED IN DETENTION, AND COUNTLESS MORE SALVAGED AND ASSASSINATED, AS. LONG AS THE INVESTMENT CLIMATE COULD BE RENDERED PLEASING AND ATTRACTIVE TO FOREIGN INVESTMENTS.

And what ideology, after all, does foreign investment represent?

From a circular issued by Sycip, Gorres, & Velayo, we are informed formally that protectionism presents multinational companies with difficulties. In brief, that foreign investments are anti-protectionist. (*Management Services*, June 1973, issued by Sycip, Gorres, Velayo & Co.)

But from Mr. Roy L. Ash, president of Litton Industries, and member of the board of directors of the Bank of America, Inc., comes this even blunter statement:

"Free trade is not enough: free international business is essential to meet the needs of the world ahead.

"To achieve free and fair business in its

broadest - and only workable - sense in today's world requires the substantial reduction of all barriers to international industry and commerce - not just the classical tariff hurdles that inhibit trade." (see Business Day, March 21, 1972, article titled "Multinational Corporations Can Best Promote World Business.)

This, in sum, is the ideology for which Virata, Paterno, et. al. justified the martial regime that they so slavishly served for more than a decade.

Paterno in fact was saying that dictatorship was necessary in order to force Free Trade on a nation which had rejected it.

In that he was right. Dictatorship, which the technocrats served, was necessary in order to continue with the economic colonization of a people who had refused to be colonized.

The Labor-Intensive, Export-Oriented programme subjected the economy to a sustained, merciless mauling, as the chain of devaluations, the massive importation of goods and the flight of capital worked out their iron process.

The devaluations desolated the people's purchasing power without creating the industries that would have compensated for the loss of the purchasing power; the free and open import policy devastated local businesses; and the policy of cheap labor reduced the working man to a condition worse than penury and destitution.

One of the most devastating consequences of the programme was the way the series of devaluations unceasingly increased the peso cost of the dollar obligations incurred by local industries. The destruction of local industries could not have been planned more systematically and cold bloodedly.

NOTHING IN THE POST-WAR HISTORY OF THIS COUNTRY HAD BEEN MORE PRODUCTIVE OF HUMAN MISERY AND MASS POVERTY THAN MARTIAL LAW AND THE ECONOMIC POLICIES THAT CAME WITH IT.

Agricultural imperialism.

Concomitant with the labor-intensive, export-oriented program came a policy of agricultural imperialism, as the agricultural sector, traditionally reserved for Filipinos, was opened to mammoth foreign agri-business companies engaged in the export of Philippine plantation crops while thriving on imported fertilizer and other foreign inputs.

These inputs became official fad, not only because the corporate plantations used them but because they constitute a major production item of foreign chemical interests which support IRRI.

The nation's agricultural system was reorganized in a way that made it dependent on these imported inputs. In the meantime, devaluation would eventually place these inputs beyond the reach of the small farmer, even as they destroyed the fertility of the nation's soil.

The privilege given to these agri-business conglomerates included that of dispossessing small fanners and grabbing the ancestral lands of ethnic minorities.

To this may be traced the explosive land problems of the ethnic minorities in the Cordilleras and Mindanao.

The dictatorship that Virata, Paterno, et. al. justified in the name of their programme created the very situation which induced, encouraged and permitted the massive plunder of the nation's treasury.

Dictatorship, as a political system, was necessary to enforce the technocratic programme; dictatorship, in turn, meant the absolute power to plunder the nation, and violate human rights in the process.

The atrocities committed by the Military are nothing compared to the human suffering which the technocrats have inflicted on the entire country through their policies.

How many lives did the soldiers maim and kill?

Two Hundred Thousands perhaps?

But how many millions of lives have been driven by the policies of the technocrats to destitution and prostitution; how many thousands of industries rendered bankrupt; how many tens of thousands made unemployed? How many millions of homes broken, and families sundered?

How measure the loss of this nation's sovereignty? How value the missed and lost opportunities that could have come with a real development program, as had been decreed by no less than Congress?

How measure human suffering of the last fourteen years in its total dimension?

But it is a reflection of the inverted values of this society that, while excoriating the plunders of Marcos and the violation by the military of human rights, the technocrats are not only spared from national security, but in fact are openly embraced by the religious and business communities.

Melchor has been endorsed by Cardinal Sin for an ambassadorship; Paterno is now back in public service. Virata has been spared the ordeal of scrutiny, and has now begun to start pronouncing on public questions; Ople has been appointed to the Constitutional Commission.

What is this but signal that the ruling Establishment, led by the government and the most prominence of the Church sees nothing wrong with the technocracy and the technocratic programme of the Marcos dictatorship; and that, in the view of the Establishment, the programme of the Marcos technocrats should continue.

This in fact is the implication of the following report concerning the support given by Cardinal Sin, reportedly on behalf of the Church, to the national recovery program of the Aquino government:

> "Manila Archbishop Jaime Cardinal Sin said Friday, the Church is supporting the national recovery program of President Aquino and urged the Filipino people to do the same.
>
> xxx
>
> "Sin said the Church, aware of the present economic crisis and the need to alleviate the plight of the Filipinos will intensify its campaign to generate more support and donations for the country's poor." ("Church Supports Aquino Program, *Malaya*, June 8, 1986).

So let us turn to the Aquino recovery program behind which the influential Cardinal Sin has reportedly thrown the support of the Catholic church.

---ooo---

VI. The Economic Programme Of The Aquino Government Based On Free Market Economics And Free Trade

The economic programme of the Aquino government promises to adhere even more closely to the philosophy of free market economics than the Marcos regime. One infers this from the summary of policy objectives underlying the programme. These objectives, as announced by President Aquino herself are: (1) promote exports and lift import controls; (2) maintain a "realistic" exchange rate; (3) control the growth of population; (4) dismantle agricultural monopolies; (5) restructure the foreign debt; (6) encourage foreign investments; (7) launch an emergency rural employment program through public works; (8) reorganize the government machinery; and (9) improve internal revenue collections.

Noteworthy, of course, is the absence of industrialization as a program objective.

The first two objectives cited above, namely the lifting of import controls and the maintenance of a "realistic exchange rate," provide the key to an understanding of the essential nature of the programme. It is a programme based on free market economics, as insisted on time and again by the IMF.

What this means in the ridiculous concrete may be gleaned from the manifold items that have been decontrolled, or now allowed to be imported, following announcement of the Aquino recovery programme.

Among these are. "beer," "hopia," "figs," "live rabbits," "soft drinks," "egg yolk," "cocks," "perfumes and lotions," "articles of personal adornment" and an absurd multitude of others.

But more ominous still is the implication of the programme for the agricultural sector. The programme has given notice that the economy will be as open to imports of agricultural products as it will be to manufactured goods.

Wheat, flour, soybeans and feedgrains are among those that can now be freely imported.

The programme means that current effort of the country to develop its own wheat, cotton and com industries, for example, will be of naught, and that this country might as well give up all hopes of developing self-sufficiency even in agriculture.

The programme will eventually liquidate not only what remains of the country's manufacturing sector but our agricultural sector as well. We shall be reduced completely to an importing economy; an agricultural country where even agriculture shall have ceased to be viable as a productive enterprise.

To illustrate this concretely, less than a month after the implementation of the import liberalization program. Agriculture Minister Ramon Mitra complained of the importation by San Miguel Corporation of 20,000 tons of feed wheat which, according to him, "deprived local com farmers of a market for their produce."

As reported by Business Bulletin, Mitra charged that the importation was "unfair to com farmers now reeling under lower prices." (Business Bulletin, July 9, 1986).

Likewise, the Philippine Cotton Corporation alleged that the "import liberalization would adversely affect local cotton producers in view of the glut in the world supply of cotton, particularly in the United States and China." (Business Bulletin, "Hike in Cotton Duty sought, PCC Pleads for protection to 17,000 farmers" issue of July 10, 1986).

One cannot help concluding that the programme has been dictated by the requirements of the United States to dispose of its huge agricultural surpluses; this means, among others, dumping those surpluses on Third World economies like the Philippines.

A special report published in South, issue of May 1986, a prestigious publication dealing with Third World matters, is revealing.

From it we learn that -

"The US agricultural department predicts global grain surpluses of 300 million tonnes by the end of this year, with worldwide food production already double that of 1984.

"The forces of superpower govern-ments, international commodity trading companies, and the huge agri-business suppliers and producers are moulding the world agricultural scene. Over the next five years the US will dump Sl.5 Billion of grain - to cut down on the nation's towering and costly food mountains - on to already overburdened world markets at rock bottom prices."

The Aquino programme will make this country easily one of the first major dumping grounds for US agricultural surpluses.

It is not hard to visualize the harsh consequences of this program on virtually every sector of Philippine society.

Its impact on the manufacturing and agricultural sectors needs no further elaboration. The programme dooms not only industries but agriculture as well.

As the government implements its emergency employment plan in the countryside, pressure will be exerted on the dollar because of the policy of liberalized imports, and this, in turn, means the progressive devaluation of the peso under the floating rate.

Progressive devaluation spells further hardship on the consumer sector, particularly on the fixed wage-eamers, as well as increased cost of production for both manufacturers and farmers.

Price support for farmers will eventually be removed because free market economics is incompatible with government price support programs.

How then will mass poverty be resolved?

Mainly, through a campaign for more donations, which Cardinal Sin has pledged, and intensification of birth control, which the programme includes among its essential elements.

The programme would be laughable if it were not for the catastrophe that is sure to come with it. Its very nature, and the mechanics of economic oppression that it will inexorably unleash, are precisely what we experienced during martial law, and which we are scheduled to experience, with even more intensity, under the Aquino government.

This is the programme which, according to Cardinal Sin, has the backing of the Church.

---oOo---

VII.   The IMPs Free Market Economics Condemned By The Vatican

What is ironic about the position of the Catholic Church is that free market economics, represented by the IMF, has already been condemned by the papal encyclicals, and recent papal pronouncements.

For example, in his trip to Newfoundland in 1984, the present Pope was reported to have issued a "stinging criticism" of economic systems that "respond only to the forces of the marketplace."

As the International Herald Tribune further reported:

> "In his remarks on economics, the pope's emphasis was on the clanger of economic systems based solely on free markets." (*Internalional Herald Tribune.* "Pope Calls for Aid to Church Schools, Is Critical of Free Market Economies" issue of September 14, 1984)

The Pope's remarks are in turn based on the historic encyclical of Pope Paul VI, Populorum Progressio, where the principle of free trade, which lies at the heart of free market economics, was explicitly criticized as "no longer able to govern international relations."

> "In other words, the rule of free trade, taken by itself, is no longer able to govern international relations. Its advantages are certainly evident when the parties involved are not affected by any excessive inequalities of economic power, it is an incentive and a

reward for effort. That is why industrially developed countries see in it a law of justice. But the situation is no longer the same when economic conditions differ too widely from country to country."

And as if to press the point further, that pope continued:

"An economy of exchange can no longer be based solely on the law of free competition, a law which, in its turn, too often creates an economic dictatorship. Freedom of trade is only fair if it is subject to the demands of social justice."

The IMF ideology is based on the law of free competition and free trade.

It is interesting to note that even among industrially developed countries, Free Trade, as insisted on by the IMF, and to which the Philippines has substantially adhered since 1962 (in addition" to prior periods), has never been practiced.

Japan, of course, is a notorious example. But even among the western powers, it is a concept more honored in the breach.

In Canada, a highly industrial country, considerable controversy has been provoked by talks of possible free trade with the United States.

According to a report by Time Magazine, the Canadian Center for Policy Alternatives, an independent research group in Canada, has warned that "Free Trade would be an economic tragedy because tens of thousands of Canadians would lose their jobs, and Canada would become a virtual American client state." (Issue of June 2, 1986, "*A Furor Over Tariffs*')

The great crime of Free Trade against the humanity of underdeveloped nations is that it drives masses of people into forced idleness, deprives them of the opportunity to develop industries producing what they import, while cultivating in them the taste for foreign goods.

Free Trade destroys livelihood opportunities.

This was what the Sakdal, Benigno Ramos, discerned as early as the 1930s. As he remarked then:

"Sa mula't mula pa. ang mga nagsakop sa atin ang nagturo na tayo'y gumamit ng mga mahal na damit, paggamit ng kubiertos, pagsakay sa bapor at sa mga sasakyang de motor, nguni't hindi naman naglagay ng mga sasakyan at kagamitang ito upang ang mga tao natin ay magkaroon ng mapapasukan at matuto ng mga karunungang ito ng bagong kabihasnan.

"Ano kaya ang mangyayari sa isang bayan na pulos na gugol at ayaw turuan ng anumang matatrabaho? *(Mga Paiak ng Luha ng Bayang Api,* Dec. 3, 1939)

This is the kind of earthy logic that has escaped the technocrats all these years.

Free Trade economics has in fact been a major factor in what Hayter has called "*the creation of world poverty*." and nothing can be more vividly illustrative of this than the Philippine experience with it.

Free Trade, forced on undeveloped countries, as it has been forced on us, constitutes the economic basis of the colonial relation.

That is why it produces what the late Claro M. Recto and Salvador Araneta described as a "colonial economy."

And in a colonial economy lies the explanation for the mass poverty in this country.,

As Araneta would remark as early as 1948, describing the colonial economy imposed on the Philippines by the U.S.:

> "While the United States may take pride in its efforts to improve public education and health during the two generations of its rule over the Philippines, there is no blinking the fact that it imposed a colonial-type economy on its ward.
>
> "Like all other dependencies, the Philippines provided its mother country with raw materials for the latter's industries and with a market for its manufactures. Industrial development in the Philippines was not encouraged." (Araneta, Basic Problems of Philippine Economic Development, published in Public Affairs, issue of Sept 1948)

Today, almost 40 years after the Araneta speech, the colonial type economy he described remains to plague us, and if our industrial development was not encouraged then, it continues to be discouraged, and even prohibited, now.

Recto was even more explicit. In his classic speech on the need for full industrialization, delivered in 1956, eight years after Araneta's, he remarked:

> "Our is an underdeveloped country and has been so for centuries. And while our economy has stagnated. our population has increased. Mass poverty and mass unemployment have been the inevitable

results." (A Realistic Economic Policy for the Philippines)

That was in 1956, exactly thirty years ago.

The counsel of those two patriots was not heeded, and we have paid dearly for ignoring their voices.

Those two patriots were the towering figures in the struggle for industrialization waged by Filipinos after the war.

In the debates over the Bell Trade Act of 1946, it was Araneta who focused attack on its free trade provision, and it was he who consistently warned that free trade would impede the country's industrialization, just as it had impeded that industrialization during the long period of direct American colonial rule.

As he then said, time and again:

"Free trade between an industrial country and an agricultural country is to the detriment of the agricultural country.

"There is no country which has been able to become industrialized without having had to protect its industries.

"Free trade means no industrialization for the Philippines. It means a backward Philippines that will be little more than an economic dependency of the United States - serving in that regard the function of a vegetable garden to an industrial state." *("Precepts We Cannot Surrender."* speech before Manila Rotary on January 1947)

Recto, in turn, nine years later, would deliver his classic speech urging the full industrialization of the country:

"Our industrialization must include

heavy industry-basic metals, power and fuel, machine tools, machinery and chemicals xxx

"Heavy industry is the basis of any industrialization. Except as part of the national economy of another, no country can succeed in industrialization without heavy industry. It is the heavy industry that insures greater potentialities for continued increase in the production of consumer goods."

As early as then, Recto pinpointed, as Araneta had done before him, the need for an iron and steel industry.

"With respect to iron and steel, there is no justification for our timidity. It is a basic need which we ourselves can easily fill."

Those passages are from a speech delivered in 1956, 30 years ago, calling for industrialization and a *"Realistic Economic Policy for the Philippines,"* as the way out of mass poverty.

---ooo---

VIII. Marcos' Admission Of Failure, Judgment of U.N. Expert Body

The climax to the technocratic programme came in 1979 when no less than Mr. Marcos himself made 1 public confession that the anti-industrialization policy of his government had been a mistake, and that the nation should fully proceed with the development of a heavy manufacturing capability.

In an address before the Philippine Business

Conference on November 16, 1979, Marcos made the following statement:

"Since the day we regained our independence in 1946 and began our march towards modem statehood, we have been repeatedly cautioned by economists of various persuasions against adopting over ambitions industrialization programs.

"I believe such words of caution have lost their validity for us today if indeed they had any validity at all in the past

xxx

'The task that remains at hand is to provide the prize at the end of the ladder. And we intend to provide that prize for each and everyone of us.

"I believe this task cannot be achieved without a full national industrialization program. And that is what we are talking about.

Marcos proceeded to say that:

'To shrink from the risks of installing full industrial capacity at this time will result in the perpetuation of an essentially import economy in this country.

And he proceeds even more meaningfully to say:

"And we are well aware of the implications of the failure to industrialize. The result will be that it will penalize domestic consumers to whom the cost of raw material inputs to production of consumer items will have to be passed." (Daily Express, November 21, 1979; Evening Post. Nov. 17, 1979)

It was then that the idea of 11 major

industrial projects was conceived.

That was November 1979.

By 1979, however, the crisis had already overtaken the Marcos regime.

And, with that industrialization speech, Marcos sealed his political doom. From then on, Virata began to be talked about as his successor.

In 1980, the Economic and Social Commission for Asia of the U.N. (ESCAP) made a formal finding that the Labor-intensive export oriented approach is harmful to the developing countries.

In a story published in the Daily Express issue of May 4, 1980, in its Business Section, we read the following:

> "Libor intensive export manufacturing is more harmful in the long run to the developing Asian nation whose government has adopted such a policy.
>
> "With this finding, the United Nation Economic and Social Commission for Asia and the Pacific it urging governments in the region to subject such a policy to reexamination.

"ESCAP said its studies show that such a policy becomes feasible only if it is made to play a complementary role to the overall capacity of building a broader based industry capable of serving a wide range of domestic needs."

No less than an expert UN body, in brief, pronounced that industrialization is necessary to developing nations, and that the labor-intensive export oriented program should serve only as a supplement to a program of industrial development geared to basic and domestic needs.

Where then do these put the technocrats

and the programme which they forced on the nation for 14 years.

But technocrats led by Virata continue to oppose industrialization.

Notwithstanding the clear policy of industrialization announced by Marcos in November 1979, Virata continued his opposition.

He continued to undermine the program with the usual technocratic talk about viability and feasibility.

Hence, in 1981, two years after the industrial program had been announced, Virata countered that the 11 industrial projects will be pursued by the government "only if the studies to be conducted by Ongpin and Carpio show that the ventures could satisfy xxx three requirements."

And what were those "three requirements'?

These are, according to Virata, "only when they are viable, they have ready financing and they have appropriate investors." (see *Times Journal,* Nov. 28, 1981, p. 11 *"Criteria sets for 11 Major Projects).*

As that story further states: "Because of this, the timetable for the 11 projects, originally planned to be completed in 1985, then extended to 1987, might be extended anew."

And then from the private sector led by Jaime Ongpin and Dr. Bernardo Villegas came a systematic opposition to the 11 industrial projects.

At that time, according to the *Journal* report, the 11 projects would have cost only $6 Billion.

That amount was what we spent in the importation of consumer and luxury goods during the years 1979-1982. It also represents a fraction of the astronomical sums invested overseas by the crony, and other, capitalists.

From the Virata statement of 1981, virtually shelving the 11 major industrial projects, one sees that Marcos by that time had ceased to be an effective president. The technocrats had taken over, and,increasingly, Virata would assert himself aggressively as prospective head of state, even as the Marcos health began its steady decline.

Marcos had realized too late the fatal blunder of his government. The Philippines, by 1979, was already too mired in foreign debt, and therefore completely at the mercy of the IMF whose policies and philosophy were being consummately served by Virata and company.

Those policies were based on one basic command: borrow as much as you can, but never industrialize.

After incurring a $26 Billion debt, this nation cannot even be credited with a respectable toy industry.

The World Bank position on the Marcos industrialization program.

Virata's opposition, as well as that of others, to the industrialization program announced by Marcos in 1979, takes off from a formal World Bank position on the matter.

In a Philippine paper which the World Bank issued in 1980, that institution argued curiously that the establishment of the major industrial projects could have a destabilizing effect on the economy.

Business Day, in its issue of June 23, 1986, reports on the 1980 World Bank paper as follows:

> "However, the World Bank rejected the government's bid to go into such large-scale industrial operations. 'Our view is that while some of these capital-intensive projects are

economically well justified others may not be, and do not harmonize well with the policy reforms' the World Bank said in a 1980 country program paper.

"The World Bank added that the establishment of the MIPs (major industrial projects) could bring about highly destabilizing effects on the local economy. " ("Business Wants to be Consulted About Industrial Projects of Government." p. 2)

Now we know who inspired Virata and company's opposition to the industrial program which Marcos announced in 1979.

The criticism against the 11 major industrial projects provoked Marcos himself to attack and describe his critics as:

"All part of a plot to insure that the country remains under the industrialized countries." (*Times Journal* "Marcos Hits Critics of Major Projects," May 24, 1982).

The Times Journal story continues:

"The President told newsmen that a delay in pushing through a major industrial project almost always results in cost increases. "He cited the copper smelter project which, he said, now costs between $400 million to $1 billion. "When I ordered a study of the project in 1967 it cost only $150 million, he said."

By 1982, three years after Marcos had formally advocated full industrialization of the Philippines, he and his Prime Minister were already at open odds with each other. Virata became the darling of the private sector, and international criticism of Marcos began to mount.

On hindsight, Marcos was dead politically after he formally espoused the industrialization of the economy.

Who is Virata?

One cannot close this episode in the nation's history without asking, who is Virata, the man who, next to Macos and Imelda, determined, with the aid of his colleagues, the course of Philippine economic history during the martial law regime.

It is known that Virata was recruited from Sycip, Gorres, Velayo, and among his first assignments was to head the then newly created Board of Investments as well as the technical panel which started the renegotiations over the Laurel-Langley Agreement.

As Chairman of the technical panel which started negotiations with its American counterpart in 1968 Virata committed the Philippine position in favor of the extension of the national treatment clause in the Laurel-Langley Agreement.

Then in 1970, Virata made clear his position on the industrialization question. In a speech before the Philippine Normal College, he listed what he described as "erosive ideas and concepts."

Among these "erosive concepts," was industrialization, against which he argued, (see *Manila Chronicle*, April 22, 1970). That was after Congress had passed the Magna Carta calling for a program of industrialization.

As a writer, commenting on the Virata statement, remarked:

"What could be the basis of the Secretary's contention that industrialization, welfare state and credit financing are 'erosive ideas and concepts'"? (Paterno N. Alcudia. "Development Trends" in *Business Day*, April 24, 1970).

Two years earlier, as Chairman of the Board of Investments, he submitted the first investment priorities plan of that body to the National Economic Council. That plan was assailed by the NEC as "having a definite bias against basic industrialization." (see *Manila Times*, May 18, 1968 in story titled "Plan Biased vs. Industry" published in the Business Section.)

Prior to martial law, Virata also spearheaded the move to legitimize a scheme that was intended to enable wholly owned foreign companies to engage in the exploration and exploitation of the nation's natural resources in the guise of service contracts.

The concept was shelved in Congress following its widespread denunciation by public opinion as an attempt to enable foreign companies to avail of parity rights beyond the terminal date of the Laurel-Langley Agreement.

Shelved in Congress, the concept of the service contract was incorporated into the 1973 constitution following the declaration of martial law.

Then, in 1972, Virata urged that the country abandon a long standing policy against becoming a member of GATT. Membership in that world body commits the acceding country to progressively dismantle its tariff system. He eventually obtained his way, and the Philippines finally joined GATT after martial law was declared.

This is the ideological profile of the former Prime Minister.

Summary And Concluding Remarks

The Philippine situation has assumed the dimensions of an international scandal, providing a text example of how a former colony has been kept effectively a colony long after it had been given its independence.

We are a classic example of a neo-colony.

If there is any point which the preceding discussion has established, it is that mass poverty in the Philippines is a direct and immediate function of colonialist policies.

Those policies represent the principal obstruction to an industrial revolution in this country; and without that industrial revolution, mass poverty will not only persist, but will aggravate with the inevitable increase of population..

In this sense, the struggle against mass poverty is inextricably linked with the anti-colonial movement, and the particular struggle against U.S. domination.

If that struggle is to be won, it must begin with a constitution that decrees not only a program of democratization but, more importantly, of decolonization and industrialization as well.

Only such a program can establish a new economic order needed to enable the nation to proceed with its industrial revolution, and the corresponding conquest of mass poverty.

---oOo---

Part Two

Elements And Principles Of A New Economic Order: De-Colonization, Industrialization And Economic Democratization

If the new constitution is to respond to the challenge of mass poverty it must trigger three processes. These are the processes of *de-colonization; industrialization; and economic democratization.*

Industrialization, on which the war against mass poverty hinges, cannot proceed as long as colonialist power and colonialist policies rule supreme. This point has been made abundantly clear by the discussion in preceding sections. It is in this sense that the struggle against mass poverty is linked inextricably to the struggle against U.S. domination.

On the other hand, the struggle against U.S. domination can be waged effectively only when both the government and the people are united in that struggle. It is a struggle which government can undertake only if it commands the support of the masses.

Defying colonialist dictates invites colonialist retaliation. And because that retaliation is bound to result in harsh consequences for the economy, a government that has no mass support won't endure. It can easily be de-stabilized by colonialist forces exploiting the hardship and impatience of the masses.

The people's backing, however, will not be forthcoming as long as they don't perceive that the hardship and cost they are called upon to assume would lead to a new economic order that is intended, and will work, primarily for their benefit. Hence, the process of dismantling the structure of U.S. domination must go in hand with the democratization of our oligarchic economy. The masses must be given a meaningful stake in the arduous struggle for economic independence and development, both of which must be made to mean not only jobs, but the key to a qualitatively better life, for them and their children; the prospect of participating in an expanding and developing economy beyond being mere wage slaves.

Only when the processes of de-colonization, industrialization and economic democratization are set in interacting and simultaneous motion can the transformation of Philippine society then begin.

The task of triggering those processes defines, in the concrete, the essential elements of a new economic order.

---ooo---

I. Under A New Economic Order, Industrialization Should Be Incorporated As A Mandatory Objective Of The Constitutional System.

In the context of the poverty problem, which has assumed the dimensions of a social disaster, and the fact that only in industrialization can that disaster be reversed, this nation has no recourse except to industrialize.

Industrialization, as a social and national objective of the most pressing urgency, should be installed in the new constitution as a responsibility of State which no administration, regardless of its ideological persuasion, should be at liberty to ignore or neglect. It should be a permanent feature of the alternative ideology.

If matters such as the security and defense of the State and the promotion of Social Justice are important enough to be constitutionalized, with more reason should industrialization be similarly treated. The security and defense of the State, as well as social justice, are illusory objectives as long as the economy is without a strong industrial base.

Even a Bill of Rights is meaningless to a people in hunger. Man's survival depends on his opportunity to work. A pre-industrial society cannot possibly generate opportunities for work in any meaningful scale.

Any society whose economic system cannot guarantee its citizens who are willing to work the opportunity to work fails them in a very fundamental sense.

Agriculture cannot absorb the vast army of unemployed and underemployed in this country, not to mention the more than 750,000 people who enter the work force every year.

We must not only industrialize. We must industrialize rapidly, and that should be enshrined as a constitutional responsibility of government.

At the heart of the industrialization process is the creation and development of the capital goods industry, and this should be stressed in the constitutional provision on industrialization.

Indonesia is the latest convert to the need for an industrial revolution, and the role which the capital goods industry plays in it.

This is reflected in the statement of Pres. Suharto when asked about his country's development programme. Suharto answered that together with agricultural development, *"we will step up industrial development so that we can produce our own industrial machinery."* (Asian Wail Street Journal, Oct. 4, 1982, "*Indonesia To Speed Up Plan for Economy, Suharto Says'*)

Unless the Philippines industrializes, and industrializes rapidly, it will be the only non-industrial country in the ASEAN by the end of this century, and the socio-political and economic implications of that are menacing.

---ooo---

II.   The Social Necessity To Industrialize Requires An Economic System Where Private Profit Shall Cease To Be The Overriding Motive Force Of Economic Activities. From Hereon, Social Needs And Priorities Should Primarily Determine The Intensity And Direction Of Those Activities. The State Must Be Directed By The Constitution To Be An Activist And Pioneer In The Industrialization Process.

The fact must be faced that private capital alone cannot live up to the challenge and requirements of an industrial revolution. The concrete realities of the Philippine situation dictate that the State be constitutionally directed to assume the kind of economic activism that characterizes virtually every government not only in Asia, but in the entire Third World. This means undertaking the role of pioneer and entrepreneur in the industrialization process. A nation in hunger cannot wait on private enterprise to create the opportunities for employment that would enable millions to survive and be saved from their degraded lives. A nation in a state of underdevelopment cannot afford to wait on private enterprise to establish those industries that would infuse steel and muscle in an economy that subsists primarily on rice and vegetables.

We have waited long enough. The prevailing economic philosophy which would deprive the State of the right to assume the functions of an industrial entrepreneur, and which would reserve these functions primarily, if not exclusively, to private capital, is a philosophy which not only ignores historical and contemporary practice but which in feet cuts into the essence of national sovereignty. For it is a philosophy which would restrain a people from exercising their sovereign right, through their government, to improve the quality of their lives.

State activism in the economy is the general, if not universal, practice in all Asian states, as the discussion in Part One showed.

Little known also is the fact that the papal encyclicals not only recognize the necessity for the State to be an activist in the economy, but actually endorses it.

Thus in *Mater et Magistra*, we find the following passage under the section on *"Private Initiative and Intervention of the Public Authorities in the Field of Economics"*:

> "First of all, it should be affirmed that the economic order is the creation of the pesonal initiative of private citizens themselves working either individually or in association with each other in various ways for the prosecution of common interests.
> "But here, for the reasons Our Predecessors have pointed out, the public authorities must not remain inactive if they are to promote in a proper way the productive

development in behalf of social progress for the benefit of all citizens."

---ooo---

III. Economic Protectionism Is A Necessary And Indispensable Condition To Industrialization. It Should Be Incorporated In The New Constitution In Order To Ensure That No Government, Even One Acting Under Colonialist Influence, Deviates From It With Impunity.

No economy graduated from underdeveloped to developed status without exercising an intense degree of protectionism that gave domestic industries control of the home market.

Protectionism has become synonymous with industrialism.

There can be no industrialization unless the State adopts it as a permanent feature of its development programmes to insulate domestic industries from import competition, particularly during the initial years of industrialization.

Tariff protection is not sufficient because tariffs do not directly limit importations; they simply make imports costly which does not deter the rich at all. Besides, tariffs are easily circumvented by means of technical smuggling or underdeclaration and are rendered meaningless by the widespread practice of foreign governments in subsidizing their exports.

The soul and essence of contemporary protectionism lie in what are known as non-tariff barriers. The most common of these is the practice of either banning completely, or directly limiting the quantity of, imports which compete with domestic industries.

For example, the United States protects a wide range of its domestic industries, such as the textile, car, steel, shoes, oil, and agricultural products, through an elaborate system of import quotas enforced through what are described as "voluntary agreements."*

Japan simply bans outright a whole range of imports.

Banning and/or quantitative limitations on imports are also effected through government intervention in foreign exchange transactions. This is a policy extensively practiced not only by Japan, but by the newly industrialized states in Asia, namely, Korea, Taiwan, and India.

We practiced protectionism extensively during the decade of the 1950s, which explains the light industrial complex that we were able to develop during that period, and which made us then the most advanced country in Asia next to Japan.

We were constrained, however, to abandon protectionism just when the economy was set for a real industrial take-off.

The need to incorporate in the constitution a provision which would make economic protection-ism a constitional policy stems from our experience. That experience has shown that powerful forces are constantly at work to commit the nation to free trade.

In feet, thought should be entertained that the constitution make it a criminal offense for any public official to influence our public policies towards free trade. In the context of our concrete situation, and historical experience, particularly during martial law, free trade is tantamount to high treason.

---oOo---

IV.   Under A New Economic Order, Labor Should Be Treated As A Partner In The Production Process And Not Simply A Commodity To Be Paid For In Wages. This Principle Is Decreed By The Papal Encyclicals.

It is accepted that the great moral flaw in capitalism is the way it deifies profit, and its treatment of human labor as an item of commerce.

It is time that capitalism in the Philippines, which professes to be moved by Christian values, be compelled to transform its attitude towards Labor, which should be accepted as a partner in production and not dealt with simply as a commodity to be purchased at the lowest price possible, to be discarded when it can no longer function, or when the imperatives of the balance sheet so dictate that it be discarded. It is by this that capitalism operates as a dehumanizing system. The papal encyclicals are clear and unequivocal that Labor should be treated as something more than a tool of production, and that social justice demands that it participates in the fruits of an enterprise made possible by its sweat.

Pope John Paul II has devoted an entire encyclical on the need for a humane treatment of Labor and of its right to share in the ownership, management and profit of enterprise.

> "The principle of respect for work demands that this right should undergo a constructive revision, both in theory and practice.
>
> "In the light of the above, the many proposals put forward by experts in Catholic social teaching and by the highest Magisterium of the Church take on special significance: proposals for joint ownership of the means of work, sharing by the workers in the management and/or profits of businesses, so-called shareholding by labour, etc." (Laborem Exercens, Encyclical Letter of Pope John Paul II on Human Work, issued 1981.)

Mater et Magistra went even further than mere profit-sharing:

> "The demand of justice referred to can be satisfied in many ways suggested by experience. One of these and among the most desirable is to see to it that the workers, in the manner and to a degree most convenient be able to participate in the ownership of the enterprise itself."

---oOo---

V.   Under The New Economic Order Steps Should Be Taken To Ensure That Big Business Does Not Absorb Small Enterprises And Monopolize Economic Opportunities.

The democratization of the economic structure requires that profit opportunities are not monopolized by big capital, and that small enterprises, including cooperatives, are protected from the unequal and overpowering competition of private monopolies and heavily capitalized enterprises.

It is basically unhealthy to see the private sector monopolized by conglomerates and mammoth corporations who operate a chain of diversified businesses many of which can be undertaken by modestly capitalized firms. This is a practice which can only lead to the further exacerbation of concentrated wealth. It is a situation which stifles individual entrepreneurship which finds itself overwhelmed by giant competitors.

The new constitution should therefore direct government to reserve to small business specific sectors of the economy where these can thrive free from the unfair and unequal competition of heavily capitalized firms.

This policy is based on the known principle

of subsidiarity. This is a principle explicitly endorsed and espoused by Pope Pius XI. It is a principle followed by a country like India which reserves a vast range of manufacturing activities exclusively for small business.

In the Encyclical *Quadragesimo Anno*, dealing with social reconstruction, Pope Pius XI explains this important principle in Church teaching as follows:

> "None the less, just as it is wrong to v withdraw from the individual and commit to the community at large what private enterprise and industry can accomplish, so, too, it is an injustice, a grave evil and a disturbance of right order for a larger and higher organization to arrogate to itself functions which can be performed efficiently by smaller and lower bodies.
>
> This is a fundamental principle of social philosophy, unshaken and unchangeable, and it retains its full truth today. Of its very nature the true aim of all social activity should be to help individual members of the social body, but never to destroy or absorb them."

In India, among the industries "reserved for exclusive development in the small scale sector" are the making of toothpaste, laundry soap, barbed wire, bolts and nuts, wire brushes, wood screws, washers, electrical wiring accessories, electrial light fittings, assembly loud speakers, battery cell tester, automobile radiators, electric homs, exhaust mufflers, zinc oxide, paints and varnishes, battery terminal lifters, leather footwear, surgical gloves, etc., to give some random examples, (see G.D. Sharma, *"How to Start Your Own Small Scale Industry"* Orient Paperbacks, 1977)

The principle of subsidarity, which "is a fundamental principle of social philosophy" according to the aforecited papal encyclical is a potent and indispensable weapon to the process of economic democratization.

The principle of subsidiarity can, and should, also be applied to de-colonize the economy.

What the Filipino private sector and the State can accomplish should not be opened up to foreign capital and multinational companies.

Industries which Filipino capital, both private and public, can establish, should be reserved for it.

---ooo---

VI. Nationalization Should Be Used Consciously As An Instrument Of Policy To Place Industries Vital To National Security Under State Control, Break Down Concentration Of Wealth, Prevent Foreign Control Of The Economy And To Enable The Government To Implement Its Socio-Economic Priorities.

In an economy characterized by concentration of wealth and economic opportunities as well as by foreign control, nationalization becomes an inescapable tool of national security, economic democratization and de-colonization. It is a tool which should be consciously applied to facilitate the pursuit of national objectives.

In Japan and Taiwan, for example, tobacco and the liquor industries are nationalized, and in these the State enjoys exclusive monopoly, deriving considerable revenue therefrom.

Basic and capital-intensive industries, which are mother to other industries and also strategic to the national security, such as steel and telecommunications, should be nationalized. Nationalization does not of course preclude the privatization of management.

Banking is one industry that should be nationalized because in the hands of private interests, it serves as a powerful mechanism for concentralizing and siphoning public wealth to private hands, and through which economic and financial opportunities are monopolized by a closed and tiny network of interlocking interests.

There can be no meaningful public planning of the economy unless and until the financial resources of the country are subjected to social control; and that control can only be exercised by the State, as the highest expression of the nation's collective personality.

Banking, one must recall, involves the virtual power to create money. That power should never be given to private interests. It should be reserved exclusively to the State.

India provides an illuminating example of how government can implement radical social reforms through the nationalization of its banking industry. In its issue of 15 January 1985, the *Asian Wall Street Journal* carried a special report on the felicitous impact of Indira Gandhi's bank nationalization program on her country's economy.

Said the report:

"Nationalizing all of India's big privately owned banks was one of the late Prime Minister Indira Gandhi's most popular moves early in her tenure.

"Sixteen yean later, the move still draws little criticism. There is wide agreement that nationalization forced the banks to serve a broader clientele and to support the country's development programs. Tens of thousands of rural branches have sprung up. Banks are required to maintain certain percentages of loans for small enterprises and farmers."

The report continues that following the nationalization of the banking system, the rural sector and small business began to get an increasing share of the national credit. Even marginal sectors of the economy began to benefit from the financial system.

The reaction of professional economists have generally been favorable, and they admit that private banks would not likely have expanded into the rural areas had it not been for government pressure.

After its nationalization India's banking system was able finally to assist the marginal poor who otherwise would never have acquired access to loan capital.

India did this through a program of social credit under which non-collateralized loans were regularly extended to the poor applying for capital to establish small businesses.

As the *Journal* report describes it:

"On appointed day unemployed people line up to receive expedited low-interest loans of 5,000 rupees unsecured by collateral. The loans supposedly are for starting small businesses such as buying a rickshaw or sewing machine, or operating a tea stall."

The principle of nationalization and state ownership of the means of production is now recognized and enshrined in papal teachings.

In the encyclical Mater et Magistra, dealing with recent developments on the social question, Pope John XXIII states as follows:

"What has been set forth above, does not exclude, as is obvious, that also the State and other public agencies should lawfully possess as property productive goods especially when they carry with them an opportunity too great to be left to private individuals without injury to the community at large.

In modem times there is the tendency towards a progressive taking over of property whose ownership is vested in the State or other agencies of public authority. The (act find its explanation in the ever widening activity which the common good requires of the public authorities to carry on."

That encyclical was issued in 1961.

---ooo---

VII. The Essential Elements Of A Real Program Of Agrarian Reform And Reconstruction Should Be Established By The New Constitution To Distinguish Such A Program From One Which Is Concerned Mainly with Land Re-distribution.

The reconstruction of our rural areas should be based on three elements. These are (1) land justice, under which land shall be owned by the tiller, (2) industrialization, under which the rural economy shall cease to be based simply on land but shall, in addition, incorporate the machine process, so that productivity becomes a function of both land and manufacturing industries, small, medium and large scale; and (3) economic democratization, under which opportunities for livelihood are opened to the powerless and not restricted to a limited few who are endowed with capital and have monopolistic access to economic resources.

The key to the implementation of the third element lies in the development of cooperatives as a democratic mode of ownership. A real program of agrarian reform must include reserving to cooperatives specific categories of economic activities. Only by such monopolies can the powerless in the rural areas be effectively induced to mobilize collectively and be ensured that their livelihood ventures are effectively protected by a monopoly status.

There is nothing wrong in giving the poor economic monopolies that would ensure them of livelihood.

This is an instance where monopolies are indispensable to economic democratization. The poor must be given monopolies provided they organize themselves into democratic cooperatives.

Areas planted to export crops, like coconut and sugar, for example, which can be cultivated only on the basis of economies of scale, should be converted into either plantation cooperatives owned by the workers therein or as state farms.

The program of agrarian reform should progressively lead towards the democratic adoption of farm collectives or cooperatives as a dominant mode of land ownership in order to promote large scale production.

---ooo---

VIII. A New Economic Order Must Be Characterized By A Constitution Which Directs The State To Evolve A Socio-Economic System That Would Guarantee Full Employment, Economic Democracy And Social Security.

A new economic order must be based on the realism that there can never be an ideal society at any given period of time. No one ideological faction can have a monopoly of the truth, nor a monopoly of the solutions.

Hence, the Constitution of a new economic order must contain a directive addressed to both government and people that they must constantly seek the equally constant improvement of their institutions in order to realize certain fundamental social goals, among these being full employment, economic democracy and social security.

This nation should cease to be a society of human derelicts, where masses are forced to languish in destructive and self-demeaning idleness, where a situation of concentrated wealth enables a few to play God to millions of starving and desperate lives, and where the aged and the handicapped must face life unassisted.

The strength of communist societies is that they are constantly seeking the material welfare and security of their members.

A society that calls itself Christian can do no less.

---oOo---

IX.   A New Economic Order Must Stress The Need To Propel The Philippines To The Age Of Science, Technology and Industry By The End Of This Century. Nationalism And The Physical Sciences Should Be The Cornerstone Of A New Educational System.

This country lags behind the new industrialized states of Asia by as much as 25 years in terms of science, industry and technology, and by as much as 100 years behind the industrial powers.

This is a condition which must be rectified immediately because we live in an age of competing nation states whose economies are based on metal and science, while ours remain based on rice, ice cream and bananas.

The key to a vigorous and prosperous future lies in the minds and attitudes of our youth, who must be equipped with the skills, the technological and scientific knowledge as well as with the intense nationalism which today characterize the surging youths of Asia.

Our educational system is producing graduates steeped in the economics of colonialism, and almost completely ignorant of the economics of nationalism and self-reliance.

The school system which produces graduates like Virata, Valdepeftas and Villegas,

Sicat and Monsod, who insist on Free Trade for a oountry like the Philippmes is proof that there is something fundamentally deficient if not outrightiy treasonous in the country's educational system.

This situation must be reversed if the educational system is to stop producing unwitting Benedict Arnolds in the economics profession.

---oOo---

X. Under A New Economic Order, Children Of The Poor Should Be Guaranteed Free Education All Through College, And The Biggest Item In The Public Budget Should Be For This Purpose.

The poor in this country are completely without the necessary intellectual capital with which to wage their struggle for life and survival.

An essential element of a social justice program is to provide free education to those who cannot afford school. This is imperative, not only for considerations of humanity and social equality, but also for national security.

We cannot be a nation of sixth graders.

There is no point talking of economic democracy where the majority of our people do not even have the intellectual capital to exploit economic opportunities.

This is a principle which does not require elaboration.

---oOo---

XI. A New Economic Order Should Constitutionalize The Need For A Democratic System Of Central Economic Planning, Oriented To The Basic Needs Of The Poor As Well As The Urgent Requirements Of The State For An Industrialized Economy.

The industrialization of the Philippines can be undertaken only on a planned basis, and cannot be left to chance or even indirect modes of governmental persuasion.

If the State is to be an activist in the industrialization process, then it should be guided by a central plan drafted on the basis of democratic consultation with the people who are after all to be the principal beneficiaries of development.

What should be remembered is that industrialization is not a simple question of protecting and encouraging existing industries, or of preserving the present structure of the industrial system.

Industrialization entails and involves the striving towards an industrial system that could and would stand on its own, with minimum dependence on external sources for its existence and viability. It entails the unceasing creation of related industries feeding on, and supplying, the requirements of each other, and linked to the rest of the economy, notably to the agricultural and mining sectors.

Such an industrial system has to be planned, and cannot be developed on the basis of free enterprise, which presupposes and decrees the negation of State intervention.

This is now the widespread practice in virtually every state in the Third World, including the tiny city-state of Singapore.

The constitution must create a central planning authority whose processes would combine the principle of democratic consultation with the groups and sectors affected by its plans with the principle of centrality which would ensure that the various and manifold policies that enter into and constitute a development program are conceived in harmony with each other, and implemented coordinatedly.

The monetary, fiscal, budgetary, import, foreign exchange, trade, science, natural resource, agricultural, education, and many other policies of the State have far too long been conceived independently of each other and explains the perennial conflict and contradictions that attend their formulation as well as implementation.

This must cease. The development policies of the State must be conceived and implemented as an integrated whole.

Such a central planning authority must also be constitutionally directed to have a program at all times designed to place the cost of basic food items housing, educational materials, medicine and hospital facilities within the reach of the low income class. Only in this way can the nation's development plans be considered truly people-oriented.

At the same time, such a central planning commission shall be expressly directed to transform the Philippines into a truly industrial state by the end of this century, with a fully developed capital goods industry controlled by Filipinos, and where the manufacturing sector accounts for at least 35% of the Gross National Product.

---ooo---

XII. The New Economic Order Must Commit Itself To The Worldwide Movement Against Imperialism And Neo-Colonialism In Any Form And From Whatever Source. The New Constitution Must Decree A Foreign Policy Based On Non-Alignment.

The constitution of the new economic order should be firmly and unequivocally committed to the anti-imperialist struggle in the Philippines as well as in the Third World.

This country has been for so long, and up to now, the classic victim of imperialism and neo-colonialism, and its struggle against these should be reflected in no less than its constitution, which is the nation's supreme political document.

Our foreign policy must be based on non-alignment in the destructive struggle of the superpowers.

And because of this commitment, the new constitution should provide for the automatic repudiation of the U.S. bases.

As long as the bases remain, non-alignment is impossible and US imperialism will remain with us.

These bases provide the U.S. government with the reason and motivation to intervene constantly in our internal affairs, particularly in our politics, thereby functioning as a divisive and de-stabilizing factor in our national life.

At the same time, these bases impede us from undertaking a foreign economic policy that would attract maximum economic cooperation from the socialist countries.

---ooo---

XIII. Other Proposals

The specific proposals so far given are not by any means exclusive, and this paper is in process of studying and formulating additional proposals.

We welcome critical and constructive suggestions from all concerned groups, and the finalization of this paper will await receipt of critical comments from the public.

I believe, however, that the materials herein presented are sufficient to constitute the working basis of a dialogue with all sectors of society, and they are being released at this time, although incomplete, precisely to invite such a dialogue and to focus the national attention to the problem of mass poverty which should be eliminated in this country by, at the latest, the end of this century.

Concluding Remarks

The struggle against mass poverty is fundamentally a political struggle. It is a political struggle against forces, local and external, which have a historical as well as contemporaneous interest in the preservation and perpetuation of those values, policies, attitudes and practices that function to suppress an industrial revolution in this country; which operate to freeze the nation's economy in its pre-industrial mold.

Unless and until these forces are overcome, this country cannot even begin the first step in the proverbial journey of a thousand miles.

This is the meaning of the anti-colonial struggle. It is a struggle waged at all levels of society to overcome the political, military, economic and social forces that are identified with the operative causes behind our perpetual state of underdevelopment and technological backward-ness.

This is the reason why the struggle to dismantle the bases, to contain the activities of transnational corporations, to resist the pattern of IMF conditionalities, to revamp the substantive content of the educational system, to establish capital-intensive industries, to maintain a control on imports and the flight of capital, and others of like nature, are actually far more relevant to the struggle against mass poverty than the campaign being undertaken by religious and philantrophic organizations for food aid, grants and donations from foreign sponsors. These are palliatives that can anesthesize a people's consciousness against colonialism if undertaken outside the context of the anti-colonial struggle.

Colonialism and mass poverty, which are inextricably linked, should be of particular concern to those with a fierce attachment to Christianity and the Catholic faith.

At the rate that the non-Christian peoples in Asia are progressing towards independence, modernization and industrialization, the Philippines could find itself by the end of this century at the far bottom of the political and economic ladder, the only neo-colony and non-industrial state in Asia, immersed more than ever in human misery and technological backwardness as well as under foreign domination.

The political status and human condition of the Filipinos will then stand in sharp and glaring contrast to the independence, the vigor, the well-being, the prosperity and the humanity of the non-Christian peoples in Asia.

By then, Christianity and Catholicism in Asia will have become synonymous with Filipino squalor, Filipino poverty, Filipino prostitution, Filipino degeneracy, and all the ills and evils associated with and brought about by colonialism and mass poverty, and the question will be raised: is there a connection between the condition of such miserable Asian people, on one hand, and their religious faith, on the other.

And what will the Christian answer, In this only Christian nation in Asia, be then?

In the meantime, the nation struggles for naked survival.

---oOo---